WHAT A THING
TO SAY

WHAT A THING
TO SAY

John Pepper

Illustrations by Rowel Friers

Blackstaff Press

Also by John Pepper

A Quare Geg
Catch Yerself On
See Me, See Her

First published in 1977 by
The Blackstaff Press Limited
3 Galway Park, Dundonald, Belfast BT16 0AN, Northern Ireland

Reprinted 1980, 1982, 1983, 1984, 1985, 1988, 1989, 1991

Printed by The Guernsey Press Company Limited
ISBN 0-85640-137-4

Contents

List of Illustrations

To all the men and women
of the Pravince
who have shown me how much
they believe in freedom of speech.

John Pepper

'Yesterday it was raining shoemaker's knives so it was.'

Amid the welter of comment about Northern Ireland in recent years surprisingly little note has been taken of the unique qualities of the speech of the people.

For some reason only sparse attention has been paid to their lively, colourful use of the Queen's English, to the fact that Ulster is a paradise for the connoisseur of the colloquial, where the idiom has qualities no less striking than those which mark Scouse, Geordie, Cockney, or Glaswegian, and where so often it is not so much *what* is said as the *way* it is said.

A woman shopper in a Belfast supermarket was heard conveying this confidence to a friend:

'D'ye see me? D'ye see m' man? D'ye see cheese? Well it makes him throw rings round him.'

Anywhere else in the world the information would most likely be communicated by a simple statement such as, 'Cheese makes my husband sick.' This serves the purpose but it fails to conjure up such a vivid picture of the man of the house and his particular dislike.

An Australian wanting to know the price of an article would ask 'Emmachisset?' No less in need of translation would be the exchanges between two Belfastwomen meeting in the street and discussing their plans:

'Wherreryefir?'

'Amferout.'

'Ferout by yir loan?'

'Aye.'

The stranger who heard them might get the impression that it would not come amiss if a notice warned Belfast Airport arrivals, 'English *nearly* spoken here.'

Not so.

1

Quite a lot of the language of the people is Elizabethan. There is a long list of words and phrases still in daily use as Shakespeare used them, expressions such as 'It's a brave day', or 'I've been thinking long'.

A Co Londonderry child asks 'Where has my cap got to?' and will talk of 'mitching school' in complete ignorance of the fact that he is using exactly the same expression as Sir John Falstaff when referring to Prince Hal.

Similarly a Belfastwoman will say of her ailing husband, 'He's a thought better this morning', quite unaware that she is following a usage which figures in *As You Like It*.

The Elizabethan influence even rears its head in kindergarten. A pupil told his teacher 'The bus bees late.'

'Bees it, indeed?' said the teacher with sarcasm.

'Aye and some days there bees no bus at all.'

The boy, of course, was simply following the practice common in many parts of Co Down where the statement 'It be to be' simply means 'What's to be will be.'

But it is better not to be too hasty about criticising what appears to be bad grammar.

At the time of the Act of Union the Speaker of the House of Commons is quoted as having said, 'We have the Scotch catched.' His language was not even considered ungrammatical let alone unparliamentary.

Certainly those who keep their ears cocked in Ulster can be assured of hearing constant usages with qualities of their own, qualities that show a distinct sense of word-power.

On a wet morning the visitor is apt to be surprised when greeted with the salutation 'Saft?' His best bet is to politely agree, even if he has no idea whatever that this is local shorthand for 'Damp, isn't it?'

The taciturn Ulsterman will often say 'Stry' rather than 'Dry kind of a day?', again to the confusion of the stranger.

'A right shower' means one that has been fairly heavy but 'An hour's heavy rain would do more good in a week now than a week's rain would do in a month later on,' voices a longing for the end of a particularly long dry spell because the crops are suffering.

'Sharp enough for two pairs of braces' is self-explanatory, although it requires some thought by the uninitiated if someone who has been away on holiday says of the weather they experienced, 'We were able to get out.'

'A wee bit of a plout' is another variation of 'The rain didn't last,' but if the word 'Spittin' ' is directed at you it means you should think of reaching for your raincoat.

'We had a wee skiff yesterday' is intended as a helpful comment on the

'Mitching school?'

weather that has passed, in the same vein as 'It's a good job you weren't here earlier for it was rainin' shoemaker's knives.'

Meteorological exchanges in Northern Ireland can sometimes lead to unexpected discussions. A Co Antrim man met a well-known local tramp trudging along on a wintry day with his shirt unbuttoned, exposing a neck that was almost blue.

'Cowl,' said the tramp.

'Why don't you fasten your collar then?' he was asked.

'No button.'

'Would you like a pin?'

'Pin? What hate is there in a pin?'

There was no answer to that.

It is no less difficult to cap the statement, 'To tell you the truth I don't mind about the weather so long as it's dry.'

But comments on the weather aren't the only hurdles facing those whose knowledge of the quirks of Ulster speech is limited. Anyone asking the way must have their wits about them if they are to make anything of the advice they receive. I have known people pretend they don't know where they are just to hear what form the answers their appeals for directions will take.

Once when I sought to establish if I was heading the right way I was solemnly advised, 'Keep right on till you come to a gable whitewashed blue and you'll be on the pig's back.'

On another occasion I was told, 'Well, it's ten minutes walk if you run.'

'It's a wee bit down the road' can mean anything up to ten miles, although not quite so far as 'It's just a bit of a dander.'

A different kettle of fish is, 'Go on up the road there, turn right, and you'll come to a high wall. Well, it's just past that coming the other way.'

When I once inquired if I was on the main road to Ballymena I was told, 'It is that, and the nearer you get to Ballymena the mainer it gets.' This assumes an awareness of the fact that the town has a reputation rather like that of Aberdeen.

The traveller in rural parts is just as liable to be told 'It'll only be a wheen of minutes till you're there' as 'Go over that hill fornenst you and its two doors abin the slap.'

Or he could be advised, 'Take the next road to the left and when you're half way to McCluskey's pub turn right.' This is fair enough provided you are as familiar with the hostelry as your informant.

'It's a fair bit' implies a formidable walk, one not to be tackled lightly, in a different category entirely from 'It's a wee while along,' or 'It's a quare bit of a lick. so it is.'

All of which shows that it is not unrewarding to lose your way although the stranger should be on the alert in case he is taken literally. This happened to the man who asked 'Do you know the right way to Millbrook?' He got the answer 'Man, I do indeed,' and saw his informant walk happily on, leaving in his wake the unspoken words, 'Ask a silly question.'

An element of local knowledge is often called for, in a situation such as that which produced the advice, 'Take the first turning on the right and follow the tar.' Some roads have a cement surface, others tarmacadam. The idea was to explain the difference.

It is advisable not to get the idea that your leg is being pulled if you are told, 'In your shoes I wouldn't start from here at all. I'd go down to the other end of the street.'

If you are instructed, 'You'd best go the orr way' it demonstrates one oddity of Ulster speech, a tendency to drop the 'th' in words with this syllable. This produces 'morr' for mother, 'farr' for father, and 'whaerr' for whether.

It explains why a Co Down youth, objecting to an outing some friends proposed in a rather battered Mini, put it like this 'I'd far rar bar the farr's car.' Whether his father did in fact lend him his car is not recorded.

'He has the pan for breakfast seven days a week.'

The place held by the frying pan in the Ulster life-style is quite exceptional. It fulfils a vital function; its niche no less firmly established that that of the saucepan in Wales.

I can never resist a feeling of warm regard for the Ulsterman who boasted to a friend, 'My missus always gives me the pan for breakfast, so she does.' What higher testimonial could there be?

A like devotion to the utensil is reflected in the revelation 'I never make dinner of a Saturday. I just fry the pan,' although running it close as a pronouncement to remember is 'You just couldn't beat the pan.'

Similar enthusiasm is shown by the disclosure, 'They tuk half my sister's stummick away and now she can ate anything. The other day she even had the pan.'

One proud mother with a son working abroad emphasised his faithfulness as a correspondent by saying, 'I could put the pan on for his letter every

Monday morning.'

Possession of an iron stomach isn't necessarily implied if you hear the statement, 'He has the pan for breakfast seven days a week,' while 'My man's just dying about dip' is another way of indicating that the gentleman has a weakness for fried bread.

The assistant headmaster of a Belfast secondary school has never forgotten his first encounter with the Ulster idiom. He had just arrived in the city after a rough crossing from Liverpool and was shivering with cold when he knocked at the door of the house where he had booked lodgings.

When his landlady saw him on the doorstep her first words were, 'I suppose you'd like the pan?'

'What,' he asked in astonishment, 'would I like a pan for?'

A short time in Ulster left him secure in the knowledge that the question was meant in the kindliest way. But if the pan is given prominence the teapot does not come far behind.

The woman who insisted 'I like my tea all milk' had her own special taste, as distinct from that of her friend who said, 'I take that little milk you wouldn't know it was tea.'

Earning a special idiomatic spot is the peremptory call to a youngster playing in the street, 'Come on in for your tea or you'll get it. It's porridge.' The first sentence implies that disobedience will bring its own punishment. The second records an aspect of Northern Irish life: that families who have porridge for their evening meal are by no means unknown.

I have heard the statement, 'I'd as soon have cocoa for my tea for it makes me sleep.' It has connotations with the pronouncement of the Belfastman who said he didn't like coffee because it didn't taste like tea.

Doubtless it was from the same source that there came the profoundly touching lamentation, 'D'ye know this? I threw the teapot out and didn't know there were a coupla cups in it.'

The invitation 'Will you have a mouthful in your hand' does not, of course, mean exactly what it says. Rather it is an invitation to have a cup where you are sitting as distinct from having it more formally at the table. One visitor, warned against interpreting the words literally, survived the hurdle until he found himself a guest at a Co Antrim farmhouse. His host thrust a bowl of hot, steaming soup in front of him and said, 'Throw that across your chest there for it'll warm the cockles of your heart.' He waited cautiously to see how the others tackled it before he did.

Just as disconcerting is a statement such as, 'He put his head round the door and there I was sittin' in the middle of me dinner.'

There is a strong Ulster preference for the indirect statement rather than the direct. Instead of saying of a person 'That fella has buck teeth' the asser-

tion will be made 'That fella could ate a tomato through a tennis racket.'
Some may challenge the claim that the statement is of Northern Irish origin.
I am convinced that it is.

What could beat the subtlety of the guest who said after an indifferent
wedding lunch, 'There was any God's amount of mustard.'?

The visitor might get the impression that he is among people with canni-
balistic instincts on hearing 'I'm away up to my mother-in-law's for a bite.'
The speaker shouldn't be taken literally any more than the person who asks,
'Will you come round tonight? I'm baking in the oven.'

Even borrowing from the people next door can be put in a disarming fashion. 'Could you lend me a wee colour of milk?' makes it a request no one
could refuse. If sugar is sought it would be 'Could you spare me what you
couldn't see?'

There are special niceties about having someone along at your house for a
meal. No offence is taken if the guest when asked 'How would you like your
egg boiled' answers 'There's a friend of mind who ate two and he's living
yet.' Again 'How would you like your egg fried?' is liable to inspire the
good-natured reply, 'With another one.'

And there is a vividness of its own about the phrase 'He has an eye like a
cold fried egg.'

Eating out is full of surprises. There was the uncouth diner who complained, 'Hi miss, this oul tea's like cowl clart.' He was asked 'Would you
like a serviette?' He replied, 'No, I'd rather have a couple of slices of
wheaten, if it's all the same to you.'

It would be difficult to find a more blistering description for the poor
quality of the food at a Belfast restaurant than the customer's 'That's soup
you could top a battery with.'

A waitress was rebuked by her employer for serving with her top dentures
missing. She complained that they were hurting her and was promptly told,
'That doesn't matter. You'll just have to get them in again when you're on
the floor.' 'Is that so?' she challenged. 'What on earth do you expect for the
pay we get here? Bunny girls?'

The rights of the individual are always stoutly defended. An Ulsterman, a
guest at a formal dinner in London, unwittingly kept placing his knife and
fork in the finished position. Twice the waiter tried to remove his plate and
twice was brushed aside.

When it happened a third time the diner addressed the long-suffering
man, 'Touch that plate again an' I'll snedd the fingers aff ye.'

The waiter wasn't to know that a familiar piece of mechanism on an
Ulster farm is a turnip snedder, used for cutting off the tops. Nevertheless
he got the message.

7

Care has to be taken that feelings aren't ruffled when there are guests in the house. One such visitor who had partaken with relish of a meal consisting of three helpings of turkey, five potatoes, several helpings of peas, two slices of apple tart, and a piece of fruit cake, all washed down with numerous cups of tea, was asked if he felt like another piece of cake.

'I would not,' he snapped. 'Do you think I'm a glutton?'

He struck me as sharing the philosophy of the lady who wanted to indicate that some potatoes she had been given were on the small side. 'Aren't they wee?' she said. 'Sure you could put two or three in your mouth at the wan time and talk to the neighbours.'

'I felt worse many a time when I was half as bad.'

'I'm feeling proper poorly' is one of the most frequently heard replies when an Englishman, consulting his doctor, is asked what his trouble is.

This wouldn't do in Ulster. There they set out to be more explicit.

This was discovered by a young GP from Yorkshire, newly arrived in Londonderry, when a woman patient telephoned asking him to come with all haste to see her busband. 'It's his head,' she explained. 'He's had it off and on all day and now he's sitting with it in his hands between his knees.'

Her concern was not unlike that of another bothered wife who complained, 'My man keeps falling off his feet with his head.'

One young medico, fresh from North London, on his first day in a Belfast hospital, made a tour of a women's ward, mainly to establish a relationship with the patients.

When he asked the woman in the first bed how she was doing she answered, 'Ach doctor, I felt worse many a time when I was half as bad.'

It was a bewildering start but he valiantly went to the next bed where his inquiry brought the reply, 'You know this, doctor, I can feel the stitches knittin'.'

He added it to the first comment as something to be translated later, only to hear an elderly lady, next on the list, explain, 'My heart's scalded, so it is.' It was a disability he had not before encountered.

At bed No 4 he received the greeting, 'You know this, doctor? That surgeon made a right hand of my leg so he did.'

By now in a slight daze, he struggled on as Patient No 5 informed him,

'He's sitting with it in his hands between his knees.'

'That night nurse is terrible. She cut me to the bone.' He looked in vain for visible signs of wounding.

From the sixth bed he visited there was another grumble about the night nurse. This time she was denounced because 'her head's too big for her boots.'

Patient No 7 was no help in making things clearer. She informed him 'I'll tell you this. I'm as well as what I was before the way I am now.'

He had almost taken flight, convinced that there was no way to a quick understanding of it all, when a woman in the bed nearest the door called him over and pleaded anxiously, 'Would you for God's sake get the nurse to hurry up with my sleeping pills, doctor? I can hardly keep my eyes open.'

In the surgery the disabilities can sound equally confusing. Women will just as readily complain 'I can't walk with my back' as 'I can't bake with my leg.' Others have been known to lament 'I can't bake with my arm,' or 'I can't bake with my head.'

One lady whose husband had received an eye injury was heard conveying the happy tidings, 'He's doing all right. He's wearing the patch off it now.'

It was said of another ailing breadwinner, 'He's not at himself. He was up and down the stairs all night with his legs.'

From Ballymena, where the speech has strong Scottish undertones, came the lady who told her doctor, 'I fell in the sheugh and dunted my hinch.' You won't find that in *Gray's Anatomy*.

Doctors also have to contend with the innate modesty of the Ulsterwoman in order to cope with problems such as that of the lady who complained of 'a terrible pain'. It wasn't giving her a minute's peace, she insisted.

'Tell me exactly where the pain is?' her doctor asked.

She looked at him in horror. 'To tell you the truth you'd have to say you weren't looking before I could show you.'

Another young English doctor who had entered into partnership with a Belfast GP ran into bother on his first night in the surgery on his own. Asked next day how he had fared he admitted it could have been worse but said it wasn't always easy to understand what was wrong with the patient. 'Tell me,' he asked his colleague, 'what part of your anatomy is your yit?'

'Yit? Never heard of it. Why do you ask?'

'Well there was this woman who told me she had fallen into a ditch and she had thorns in her yit.'

A knowledge of Ulsterese would have left him in no doubt that the lady's problem was that the thorns were still there.

There is a uniquely persuasive ring about the advice given to a Co Armagh man, who had been complaining that he wasn't well. It ran, 'You should get down on your knees and thank God you're on your feet.'

An intimate knowledge of the idiom is an absolute essential to a chemist. He can be faced in succession with requests like:

'Could I have something for the wee lad's face? He's had it this long time and it's spreading so it is.'

'My wee girl's vomiting through a hole in her shoe. What'll I give her?'

'I want something for my husband. He has a wheezle and he's very durbley on his feet.'

'It's about this wee girl of mine Her face has broken out through her stomach.'

Few other districts could produce the query inspired by the news that a woman who had been laid up had made a good recovery but stumbled and fell and had to go back to bed with a badly sprained ankle.

'Was she lying when she fell?' was the question.

Later, when her recovery was complete, the information was conveyed by the statement, 'This morning she washed her face and hands on her feet so she did.'

It would not be easy to equal the note sent by a Co Armagh mother to explain her child's absence from school:

'Mary hasn't been because she hasn't come but the doctor has given her a dose and when she's been she'll come.'

But the tone was a trifle sharper in another parental missive to a Belfast teacher, 'Would you let my wee lad get to the toilet when he wants, not when you want?'

'A body would be better dead if they had their health' is one of those intimations you have to think out, just as 'My husband's bad' indicates merely that he is unwell, not that the rapture has left the marriage.

'If you don't put that wee jug down I'll give it to you.'

To many journalists the taxi driver is a valuable source of local atmosphere. New York's taxi-men have earned a massive number of column inches of press space through talking to visiting newspapermen.

In Belfast, while the taxi-men are not without their value to newsmen, it can be a lot more rewarding to pay attention to what the ladies have to say — if at times it can prove a shade bewildering. The point is that they are unrivalled in illustrating the wildest eccentricities of Ulster speech.

11

If a mother tells a youngster who persists in playing with something easily breakable, 'You've been polluting me all day. If you don't put that wee jug down I'll give it to you', bribery is not the intention. The real objective is to threaten severe punishment and the child knows it.

A parent chastising a child, using the words, 'If you don't behave yourself I'll pull your ear the length of your arm', would start most visitors marvelling. It would be the same if they heard the warning, 'If you don't conduct yourself I'll draw my hand across your face.'

A visitor would also be stopped short if he heard a Belfastwoman telling a friend 'You needn't dress yourself' as they prepared to go out. But it is not a suggestion that the lady should appear in public in the nude, just that she should come as she is.

It is wise not to jump to conclusions on hearing a Co Antrim woman tell a friend, 'I just got sick of him yammerin' away there, so I told him I was away upstairs to throw myself down.' Her intentions were not suicidal. All she meant was that she had gone off to bed.

Nor did the woman who 'put her feet up for five minutes and fell over' actually injure herself. She had merely dropped off to sleep.

She was clearly as worn out as the one who complained, 'I haven't sat down since I got up.'

'Wait a minute till I throw on me,' is another way of indicating that something suitable for street wear is being donned. The same motivation inspires, 'Get on your one end there and get on you.'

This usage caused some confusion to an overseas athlete at a Belfast tournament. As he was pulling on his track suit he was asked, in the kindliest possible way, 'Are ye gettin' on ye?'

By the same token 'Sit down and get aff ye' is an invitation to remove your coat and stay a while.

It is easy to appreciate the dilemma of the proud owner of a new dress who lamented, 'It was awful nice. It would have fitted me if I could have got it on.'

A different kind of comment is implicit in 'You could feel the heat of that coat the minute you take it off.'

Reflecting her own special tribulations was the woman who said, 'I wish to goodness my man was off his back till I get off my feet.'

And on the subject of women, 'She was sitting in the bus with her mouth open like a 2 lb jampot,' is a comment that seems particularly appropriate for a lady. Anywhere else it might have been just a jampot, perhaps even a 1 lb jampot. In this case the speaker was emphatic that it was a 2 lb one and the lady concerned instantly acquired a special dimension of her own.

It is not uncommon for a Co Down complaint to run, 'That oul winda cleaner of ours thinks all my windas are port holes.'

I am assured, though, that Londonderry was the origin of the grumble, 'My man came home last night at two in the morning and told me to wake him at dinner time for his breakfast.'

There the reply to such a statement is liable to be a sympathetic 'Aye, surely' which indicates the fullest understanding of the lady's problems.

Street encounters produce unexpected results all over Ulster. One woman who was sure she had seen the person involved somewhere before declared, 'I knowed I knowed her and I knowed she knowed me.'

Meetings can produce such strange confessions as 'I didn't know it was you till you spoke,' or 'Divil the bit of ye I knew till I lucked at ye.'

There are other variations.

For example, 'She never spoke and I never answered her. I never took her under my notice.'

When running into a friend the inquiry 'How are you doing?' can bring a reply like, 'It's all that's left of me after how bad I was.' No further peg is needed to launch into a detailed catalogue of the speaker's ailments.

Relations can often be oddly described. 'He's married on a cousin of mine,' indicates that he is one of the family, quite unlike the undertones of 'They're not friends. I just *know* them.'

No room for misunderstanding is left by statements like, 'I knew she was a plaster the minute I set eyes on her,' 'She can be very cuttin'' when she likes,' or 'She's nothing but an ignorant gaunch.'

Husbands come in all classifications and are favourite topics for street corner gossip. Ulster is no exception to the norm.

'I saw him measuring the walls on his way home last night,' describes a drunk. In the more acceptable class is, 'There's one thing about that oul fella of mine. He'll ate anything so long as it's fried.'

Ulster ladies are as keen on window shopping as ladies everywhere, and a particularly good comment involved a dress shop window in the moments before the shapely dummies had been draped with the garments on offer. One shopper was seen to point indignantly at the array of unrobed figures and exclaim, 'Just look at that. There's your Belfast christianity for you.'

A woman who suggested that a window model bore a striking resemblance to a mutual friend replied, 'I couldn't rightly say. I've never seen her stripped so I haven't.'

Notes left by housewives for tradesmen in Ulster follow their own highly individualistic pattern. I have been told of these examples:

'Please leave no more milk as I will be away till I get back.'

'Two pints every day till I stop it.'

'Leave thee.'

'Please knock and oblige.'

'You left me noan yesterday and I had to brow all over the place.'

'Only leave one bottle. We're not all there.'

Easily understandable is the indignation of the pinta customer who said, 'The milkman's been and gone and never came.'

Perhaps I have given the impression that Ulsterwomen have tongues as sharp as knives, but the fact is that kindliness often shines forth like a beacon in feminine utterances. No invitation could have greater warmth than, 'You're welcome at any time whether I'm in or out.'

But misunderstanding can arise so easily. I can well believe that the shop-keeper concerned is still a shade bemused over a visit from a lady in distress. He sold electrical goods and she walked into his shop and asked, 'Is this where they fix pictures?'

He felt she must be mistaken and explained that there was a chemist's a few doors along where photographic work was done.

She thanked him for his help and had just reached the door when she turned and sail chattily, 'The sound's all right but we can't see anything.'

Or maybe he isn't all that bemused. Perhaps he has shrugged his shoulders and put the lady in the same category as the one who announced firmly, 'I saw his face on the Woodstock Road.'

There is certainly no scarcity of women with a capacity for creating confusion in Northern Ireland.

They will announce 'Tell yourns ourns is for goin' ni,' to emphasise that everyone is ready for the start of a journey, just as easily as they will speak of a neighbour living a few doors down the street as 'that wee woman below me,' or describe the prospects of an early encounter with a friend in the words, 'If I don't bup you'll bidoun so don't blong.'

'My wee lad found a marley in the trinket.'

The woman diner in a Co Fermanagh restaurant who grumbled, 'That coffee tasted just like soup' was simply resorting to the exaggeration to which the indignant are universally prone.

However there was a distinctly Ulster touch about the form of protest used by a Belfast holidaymaker in Spain. She had inquired the price of a hand-bag. The shopkeeper, who happened to pride himself on the increasingly

14

broad knowledge of English he was acquiring from his customers, said 'I'm almost giving it away for nothing. Five thousand pesetas.'

She looked at him for a moment, exclaimed, 'You're a quare geg', and in an instant disabused him of any idea that his English was all that comprehensive.

It is only in an Ulster shop that the prospective customer is liable to be asked, 'Are you gettin'?' One visitor, unaccustomed to this way of asking if she was being looked after, answered, 'Gettin? No, I'm Robinson.'

A variation is the inquiry 'What might your trouble be?' A shopper to whom this question was put answered, 'Trouble? I have no trouble. I'm in perfect health.'

An incident likely to occur only in an Ulster post office happened in Belfast's GPO. A woman was seen on her hands and knees searching anxiously on the floor. A concerned observer, an Englishwoman, asked 'Is anything wrong? Can I be of help?'

'It's all right' came the reply. 'A stamp fell on me.'

The inquirer retreated in alarm, desperately trying to work out how a stamp could be so lethal, unaware that the woman had simply dropped it.

As it happened it was just as well she failed to overhear the request at a nearby counter. A woman had asked, 'Could I have a form for your teeth down the toilet?' which meant she was seeking compensation for the loss of her dentures in unfortunate circumstances.

There are qualities not everyone would instantly understand about the small boy whose mother boasted, 'He found a marley in the trinket.' He was obviously a child who kept a close eye on the gutter.

Nor would many realise what had happened if she explained, 'And it was just after he cribbed his toe on the cribbin'.' To add to the confusion it wasn't long before 'He came home again gowlin' his head aff because he got a skelf in his wee thumb.'

There is typical Ulster candour about the criticism, 'One thing sticks out about that fella. A lick of carbolic soap wouldn't do his tongue a bit of harm.'

And the effectiveness of the indirect statement is shown by the reply to an inquirer who was curious over high jinks in the town hall and asked, 'What's going on. Is it a dance?'

'I don't rightly know,' she was told, 'but I can tell you this. You need a fur coat to get in.'

The lady who went for a walk 'four nights running' earns her own special accolade, and one should go to another for her assessment of two male acquaintances. Of one she said, 'He's that quiet so he is. Sure he comes into the house like a drop of soot.' Of the other, 'He's awful well educated. He always pulls up the legs of his trousers when he sits down.'

She further demonstrated her expertise in the vernacular by announcing 'I thought I was sent for' after death has missed her on the road by a whisker.

Let a member of this articulate sisterhood loose in London and all kinds of difficulties would automatically follow. One of them had a busman stumped when she asked him 'Thissus?'

'Thissus?' he repeated. 'I never heard of it.'

How was he to know that he was being confronted by someone who scorned the straightforward 'Is this where I get off?'

It is easy to picture the reaction in Kensington if a passer-by was stopped under the impression that she was someone else, to be asked, 'You usen't to come from Omagh usen't you?'

And a discussion between two people in fluent Urdu would be as intelligible in a London tube carriage as this cosy chat between two women from Belfast:

'See this cardigan I'm wearing? I knitted it outa my head. I knit everything outa my head.'

'You must have a quare head for the knitting.'

Ulster women never seem to consider promises or threats sufficiently emphatic without the addition of the words, 'I have a good mind' to do whatever is involved. This produces such declarations as:

'I have a good mind to do nothing about it.'

'I have a good mind to do something about it.'

'I have a good mind to write to the paper about it.'

'I have a good mind to give her a piece of my mind.'

'I have a good mind to ignore her.'

'I have a good mind to start stopping paying him any more.'

Admonitions can take forms which sound strange if you don't speak the language. Only a child brought up in Ulster would understand the warning 'If you wear your bare head you'll only get your shade wrecked.'

Ulster shares with Scotland the usage of 'shade' to mean the parting of the hair; the word coming from watershed.

Scots again would have a perfect appreciation of the words of the Belfast-woman who had a chastening encounter with the customs on returning from a shopping trip across the Eire border.

'Them customs men are a sleekit lot,' she said bitterly. 'They even took the stockings I had tied round my waist.'

There is a vividness of its own about the description of a sports jacket considered unduly loud, 'It would cut the eyes out of you so it would.'

Candour is constantly in evidence in spite of the Ulster tendency for reticence. This was demonstrated by the Belfastwoman who hospitably

16

invited two overseas students to a Christmas meal.

In the course of the evening she complimented them on the excellence of their white, gleaming teeth. She was clearly envious.

'But,' said one of the guests, 'You have excellent teeth yourself. Really excellent. Are they your own?'

'Yes indeed,' was the reply. 'And I can show you the receipt.'

And when it comes to frankness it would be a hard task to improve on, 'There he was stannin' there with his two arms the one length and not a mute outa him, and her with a face on her like a well-skelped backside.'

In the same mainstream of vivid language is the confession of a Belfast-woman to a neighbour:

'We're heart scalded with the wife's farr. Last week there he was for kickin' the bucket. Friday he was bravely. Be Saturday there was no howlin' him. On Sunday he was up agin it and he had us up the pole the whole night long. Be mornin' he wanted two fried eggs. Two. As like as not be next week he'll be haughlin' away intil town as large as life and twice as natural. Cud ye bate it?'

'If he'd lived another week his wife would have been a year dead.'

'What time did he get away?' is an inquiry normally related to the time someone left on a holiday, or a motoring trip.

In Northern Ireland, while it certainly reflects an interest in departure, it has to do more specifically with departure from this life. It is one way of asking when a death actually took place; the implication being that the deceased had finally escaped from the agony of his last hours on earth. Everyone is a fatalist.

No less unusual is a way of answering the question. This could run, 'He died in the best of health. If he'd lived another week his wife would have been a year dead.' Strangers are just left to work it all out.

Idiomatic oddities relating to bereavement made no small impact on a visitor from Gloucester who had flown over to attend the funeral of a Belfastman he met on holiday. A close friendship had developed.

When he set out for Ulster he was convinced he had a fair knowledge of English. He returned home a chastened man.

On reaching the street where his friend had resided he encountered two others as uncertain as he was himself about the actual number of the house he sought. He stood by listening with interest as they knocked at a door and gravely asked the woman who appeared, 'Is this where the dead man lives?'

'It isn't,' she answered, 'it's three doors down further up.'

They thanked her, said they had come to offer their condolences, and inquired if she knew what actually caused their friend's death.

'I don't rightly know,' she replied, 'but it was nothing serious.' Then she added, a woman bursting with information, 'I went up to see him only yesterday and there he was — gone.'

'D'ye tell me that now?' one of the men exclaimed.

'Right enough,' the woman said, 'he hadn't been at himself this wee while.'

Still in a state of some confusion the visitor eventually found himself in the home of the deceased. It was crowded with mourners, all talking in low tones. The trouble was that the scraps of conversation kept adding to his bewilderment.

'I saw him a week ago and I said to myself "He's not going to do so he isn't," that's what I said.'

'He was a great friend of Big Jimmy's. Jimmy was very respectable. I was at Jimmy's funeral and there wasn't a cap to be seen.'

Then the man from Gloucester felt a tap on his shoulder and a hoarse voice whispered into his ear, 'The corpse's brother wants to know what are ye havin'?'

A glass of whisky having been thrust into his hand he was solemnly invited to 'drink the health' of the deceased.

He was thanked profusely for having travelled all the way from Gloucester to 'pay his respects' and when he spoke of the friendly relations established in such a short time with his departed friend was told, 'Ach sure enough he was a right fella was Harry. Sure you never would have heard his name mentioned.'

Here, it seemed, was the ultimate in compliments. This was not a man to thrust himself into the limelight at every opportunity, not one to make himself heard at all costs, but a person who kept himself modestly in the background, never other than unobtrusive.

It gave the visitor yet another insight into the Ulster character.

As he moved round the room he heard one mourner tell a companion, 'The wife was telling me only last week that if God spares her she's going to be cremated.'

'Is she?' came the reply. 'I have a cousin in Dublin and she had the same notion only she was told she'd have to be brought up to Belfast for they don't do any cremating in Dublin. "If that's the case," she said, "they'll have to bring me up by bus for the train makes me sick." '

Quietly the visitor moved away, to be addressed by someone who had been to the inner room where the deceased lay in his open coffin, 'You could see that that wee holiday he had a coupla weeks ago did him a world of good. You could tell.'

Another mourner immediately commented, 'I saw him only a month back. He was very annoyed when his sister died.'

The stranger wasn't to know that the word was being used in its original sense, implying considerable grief, rather than the more or less minor irrition it now usually signifies.

Someone else voiced surprise that when she called at the house to ask 'How's Harry?' 'There they were, sitting waiting on him.'

It was at this stage that the mourners were told 'refreshments' were available. In Ulster this usually means sandwiches, or bread and butter and ham, besides spirits, beer and stout. The word is all-embracing.

The Gloucester guest was about to help himself when one of the hostesses said, 'Don't be afraid of the butter.' He gave it a careful look, wondering wildly if this was an occasion when an incendiary did not lurk under the dish.

A further surprise was in store when he went along next morning to join the cortège.

A member of the family mentioned that they would be passing the building where the deceased had been employed most of his life. 'They're walking him past the factory,' he added.

'Are they?' asked the astonished visitor, picturing the prospect of the corpse being taken from the coffin for the purpose. But he was now at the stage where nothing about the obsequies could surprise him. However, it merely meant carrying the coffin until the factory was passed. But the visitor's relief was short-lived, for while he was walking along beside the other mourners the question was suddenly put to him, 'Seeing you've come such a long way maybe you'd like a lift?'

He had no way of knowing that he had merely been invited to take a turn as a pall bearer.

He went back to English-speaking Gloucester convinced that the words in the song about Galway Bay — 'They speak a language that the English do not know' — applied no less to other parts of Ireland.

It was perhaps just as well he did not share the experience of the shop-keeper who was knocked up in the early hours and found the caller to be a boy who said, 'I want a blind for a dead woman.'

Put differently he was in search of a window-blind for a house in which there had been a death. Pulling down the blinds is an essential part of the ritual of mourning. In this case they were obviously a blind short.

Another lugubrious comment the visitor missed was the one about the man who was so consistently stubborn that it was said of him, 'That fella's as stiff as Willie John's father when he was ten days dead.'

'A far worse speaker would have done only we couldn't get one.'

The individual of whom it was said 'He has a mouth like a torn pocket' could have been Protestant or Catholic. A distinctive feature of the Ulster idiom is that it crosses all divides. The vernacular is common to Methodist, Presbyterian, Roman Catholic, Episcopalian. Whatever your persuasion, the language is the same.

Religious upbringing, for example, has nothing to do with the philosophy which brought this sound piece of advice, 'I told the shopman my wee dog wouldn't ate anything but Pal. He told me, sure if you tear the label off the tin the dog won't know the difference.'

The same applies to the husband whose wife said of him, 'He has a speng in his loins and he's started walking with a wee halt.'

Indeed it is no less intriguing an exercise to try to picture him alongside the man who was 'No bother except that he tired easily when he slept.'

Character assassination seems to come naturally in Ulster. The air is constantly filled with such appraisals as:

'If you spoke one wrong word till him you'd get your head in your hands.'

'He has a stummick like an elephant. He sat down till a big fog feed and gorged himself with a clatter of champ and scallions and then tuck the drooth aff himself with a good dram of buttermilk.'

'If he died with that face nobody would wash him.'

'Her! Sure her wee lad was sent home from school because his head was walking.'

Nor is a compliment intended when it is said, 'That woman would start a fight in an empty house.'

'He's failed' doesn't mean that the person concerned has gone bankrupt. Just that he has lost weight.

'He's a rare turn' indicates that he is highly entertaining, always good for a laugh.

'If you tear the label off the tin the dog won't know the difference.'

'He has a heart of corn' is simply another way of saying he is generous to a fault, the salt of the earth, so big-hearted 'he would give you the sleeves out of his waistcoat.'

A young woman who always seemed to be overlooked when partners were being chosen at a local dance said, 'Sure them I wud hae wudna hae me and them that wud hae me I wudna hae.' Which surely not only summed up the situation to perfection but did so with dignity.

There are occasions when paying a compliment seems to involve difficulties. Votes of thanks are fraught with danger in Ulster.

A visiting preacher was once assured, 'A far worse speaker would have done only we couldn't get one.'

Another was told, 'You were far better than the clever speakers we usually have.'

Going to bed and getting up also have complications of their own.

An early caller opened the door of her friend's house in Belfast and shouted 'Are you in?'

'Aye,' came the answer, 'I'm up but I'm not down.'

Again, a woman finished a doorstep chat with a neighbour with the words, 'I'll have to go in now an' rise.' She meant, of course, she wanted to dress rather more carefully.

The same lady is on record as having confessed, 'What would suit my man down to the ground would be a nice sittin' down job where he wouldn't be on his feet all day.'

He had the same deficiency as the small boy whose father was having difficulty in finding him a job. One day a friend called and mentioned that an acquaintance in a nearby town, a tailor, was looking for an apprentice.

The boy was duly taken along for an interview, the tailor was satisfied, and the boy was launched on his new career.

Soon after his father's friend again visited the house and was surprised to see the boy running around as usual. 'What's wrong?' he inquired. 'Isn't he at his work?'

'Sure he had to give it up,' the father said. 'He just couldn't stand the sittin'.'

Constantly the desire seems to be to give bite to what one has to say, to make it sound striking rather than mundane. The dramatic statement is always preferred to the ordinary. Evidence of this is continually to be encountered, in all kinds of circumstances. It is impossible to be certain when it will arise.

A motorist filling his tank at a country petrol station one Sunday morning started chatting to the station's owner.

'Quiet here on a Sunday morning,' he said. 'Peaceful.'

'Aye,' was the dry answer from the garage man. 'But you should be here when they get out of that church across the road.'

'How come?' the motorist asked.

'It's like all hell let loose so it is.'

Actually the garage man's outlook is not unlike that of the Ballymena man once asked by a naturalist, 'Tell me, do you ever by any chance see any golden eagles around here?'

The man thought carefully for a moment, then said, 'To tell you the truth you wouldn't clap eyes on one of them for years and then all of a sudden they're trippin' you.'

Away from home the attitude is retained. A member of a Northern Ireland party of athletes competing in London was asked, 'Did you bring your own coach?'

'No,' was the serious answer. 'We came by tube.'

An Ulsterwoman will see someone in the street she thinks she knows and say wonderingly to herself, 'Now who's this thon is?'

So often a pronouncement will suggest a desperate anxiety to communicate precisely what the speaker feels. This results in the words acquiring in urgency what they lack grammatically.

A young factory worker was being rebuked by her overseer. 'Didn't I tell you you'll have to turn out better work than this?'

'You did,' said the girl. 'If a cud a wud. When a cudn't how cud a? A cudn't do it any better than a cud, cud a?'

The logic is irresistible.

The tribute can be as colourful as the downright insult. Compare 'She'd turn the house upside down to find you a shirt button' with 'If she was a field divil the crow would light on her.'

The *non sequitur* persists, however, as was indicated by the woman complaining about the barking dog owned by the people next door. 'Them people should be in when they're out to hear that dog of theirs.'

'It came to me when I wasn't thinking,' is a common form of being modest, while an indictment which can summarise a chronic weakness runs, 'She just opens her mouth and lets it say what it likes.'

The woman who said, 'I'll have to run for it's a good walk to where I'm living now,' created the impression of having something in common with the lady heard to say, 'She has four pair of boots she's never had on her back,' and subsequently confided to a friend, 'The last couch we had was a sofa.'

'He hadn't a scratch on him but he was cut to the bone.'

Listen to a typical Belfastwoman in full flight. All she needs is an audience; especially one from which there won't be too many interruptions. Communication comes as naturally to her as folding the arms. The range of her rhetoric is measureless.

In one case her audience was a neighbour who resorted to a familiar Ulster defence in such circumstances. This is to repeat the last word of the speaker's third or fourth sentence. It establishes that you are not just a nonentity, emphasises that it is not a brick wall which is being addressed.

'Hello Maria, I'm just waitin' on the wee lad to come home to give him his dinner. He's away coggin' his ekker from Aggie's wee girl. She's an awful clever child. Mind you the wee lad's smart enough if only he could put it down on paper. He takes after his grandfather. They always said of him that he wasn't much of a talker but he was a great thinker.'

'Thinker?'

'Aye. I'll say this, he's big for his size. Know what he got up to the other day there? Walked right through a glass door in one of the big shops. He hadn't a scratch on him but he was cut to the bone. You should have seen him.

'A woman said to me he was old for all the age he is but I wudn't know. All I can tell you is that there's times when he had me harrished to death. All he does is ates and ates and ates. Still, he cud be a lot worse.

'I suppose it runs in the family. Like Minnie Mehaffey's nose. Take our Aunt Lizzie there. She's been as broad as Nellie's dresser as long as I can remember. It wudn't be so bad havin' her at the house of an evening if it wasn't for the price of food. I had my man's bror over the other night there and I offered him a plate of them biscuits I bake myself. I had to ast him twyst and when he tuk one he ses to me he ses, "This'll finish me." I cud have cut his throat. Saying a thing like that about one of my biscuits. Full of curns they were, too. I'm dyin' about curns.'

'Curns.'

'Aye. Take our Lily. She cudn't boil an egg and when she makes a cup of tea ye cud stand on it to make a speech. She was terrible bad a couple of weeks ago there. Tuk a brash and nothin' wud lie on her stummick. I was that sorry for her. She went all to scrapins.'

I don't much like the luk of that day so I don't. The heavens cud open so they cud. If I cud only see enough blue sky to make an apron it could turn out all right, mind you. But then you nivver know.'

'Know.'

'Mrs Sloan, the woman above me, went to the Isle of Man on the boat for her holidays. She thought it was ratten. A waste of good money. She towl me there was nothin' to luck at for hours but the oul water. She's different to that sowl livin' opposite. She's that cowlrife she sits half-way up the chimley all day. She tuk it intil her head that her heart was bad so the minister came roun' to see her. It was the new man. Yud wud take your dead end at him. God help him, his collar didn't fit him, and he lucked for all the world like a mouse peekin' out of a white jampot. I was in stitches.'

'Stitches.'

'That's right. Me and the oul fella went to see his cousin Arter the other night there. Well he's a far out cousin. Or maybe not all that far. He's the one they used to call funky knuckles at school. I just can't take to him. I nivver cud. I cudn't tell you why. Mind you, for one thing he came to the dure in his galluses.'

'Galluses.'

'He wud remind you in a way of my oul Aunt Matilda. Her man died, remember? He tuk bronical. She nivver ast me had I a mouth on me the night I went round. What d'ye think of a woman like that? It's no wonder people always take a scunner at her.'

'Scunner.'

'Aye. But then the oddities are everywhere, so they are. There's big Joey who lights the lamps. There's nathin' he hasn't done. He was a sailor for a while but he cudn't stick it. He didn't like it, he said, because he wasn't able to go to the corner for the paper in the mornings. He got a bottle from the doctor onct and when he went back the next evenin' for another the doctor ast him where it had all gone. Ach, he said, sure the oul woman palished the sideboard with it. The same woman's a wee slip of a thing, isn't she? Ye'd wonder what happens to all she ates. She hasn't as much on her as wud keep the flies aff the sugar bowl and that's the gospel truth.'

'Truth.'

'She kept a wee shop for a while but it didn't pay. Did you know that? She gave it up. I mind somebody tellin' me onct a wee lad went in and ast her for a penth of mixed caramels. She give him two and told him to mix them himself.'

'Himself.'

'Take her married bror. He nivver bors. A modest wee man, mind ye, but he has a lot to be modest about. I'll say this. He wud nivver refuse a drink in case he offended ye.'

There is every reason to believe that the lady had a pretty close relationship with the woman in a dentist's chair, who kept up a non-stop stream of talk as he tried to work. Finally he delivered the stern warning, 'If you don't keep your mouth shut I'm never going to be able to get this tooth of your out.'

'Wud ye wait till I red the table an' rench the dishes?'

Sometimes the question arises if it is town or country which makes the biggest contribution to colourful speech. In Ulster, at a rough guess, it would be a rural victory.

It would be at a country cross-roads, not a street corner, where one would be most likely to hear, on the approach of one of the more venerable residents, 'Here's oul Harry pechlin' along. Sure there's more life in Harry's walkin' stick than there is in Harry.'

A townsman would be unlikely to say of a cleric, 'He makes his livin' by the wine of his mouth,' and the chances would be that it was a country-woman who first paid the tribute, 'Her teapot never colls.'

The lament 'The oul rheumatism's at me', and the grumble, 'The wee lad went an' tore his but of a good coat,' have an agricultural flavour, and it was certainly in a country bus that this snatch of conversation was heard:

'D'ye know William James?'

'Aye, him and me knows other.'

But country exchanges, of course, are usually to the point. The unnecessary word is avoided like the plague:

'D'ye mind him?'

'Aye, a mind him well.'

'So do I. I mind him too.'

The criticism made of a farm labourer 'He's bad on his feet' did not imply that he was an indifferent performer on the dance floor.

Similarly, the man who announced 'I haven't come till myself yet' was doing nothing more than making it known he wasn't fully awake.

Rural origins are obvious in the statement, 'Her granny was a Doherty and wore a tin hat.' This implied that the lady's antecedents were, to say the least, abnormal.

The man who said 'The wife's lyin'' was not implying that her word was not her bond; just that she was unwell and in bed.

It is usually a farmer's wife who will tell an unexpected visitor 'Wud ye wait till I red the table and rench the dishes?' Women 'red' and 'rench' in Belfast, it is true, but not to the extent they once did.

'A haitey go to the funeral' is a statement which indicates nothing more than the speaker feels it is incumbent on him to join the cortège.

Country people excel at the biting assessment.

It is easy to picture the man said to have 'a smile like last year's rhubarb'. So is the person of whom someone said, 'If it wasn't for his ears his hat would be round his neck.'

Emphatically the verdict of a countryman, usually the connoisseur of an acceptable cuppa, is 'That tea's not right drew.'

Should that be a statement which pulls you up how about 'Give us a wee lock' which is not intended to call for extra reinforcement for the door. Lock is another word for amount, as in 'A wee lock of sugar' or 'A wee lock of coffee.'

In the same way the man who 'let out a gulder' did not speak in a whisper, rather the opposite, and the politician referred to as 'Oul thundergub' was, naturally, not a man who keeps his voice lowered.

'I'll give my face a lick' needs no translation although the occasion arises when people don't always have as sharp an awareness of what they want to say. They can easily go to other extremes.

This was the case when a woman in a Co Down village went to see her doctor.

'How are ye keeping?' he asked.

'I can't say a word,' she answered.

'Your husband will be glad to hear that,' came the comment.

A countrywoman accused of being 'a puke' is considered to be a snob, sometimes a gossip. The word has an equally uncomplimentary connotation in the sentence 'He was puking', meaning he was being violently ill.

There is no significance about the news given to a caller 'The wife's at the jawbox.' This is merely the kitchen sink, one of the many words of Scottish origin used in Ulster.

It would be safe to say that dental surgeries in the country are a source of much richer exchanges than in those of the town.

'Did it hurt?' a Co Tyrone woman patient was asked.

'Just a wee notice' she answered.

A country hardware store was the setting for an incident involving a shopper in search of wire netting to keep birds from his chimney. He was insistent on solid assurances that the product he was offered would be sufficiently strong for the purpose.

Finally the shopkeeper told him, 'I'll tell ye this. If them birds cud get through that their jaws would be brave and sore so they would.'

'She's as straight up and down as a yard of pump water' is a description of someone inordinately thin commonly heard in country districts. In fact it is also heard in Yorkshire.

Certainly rural superiority is emphasised by the farmer whose horse dropped dead on the last furrow of a large hilly field which was being ploughed. With regret, the farmer regarded the body of his faithful servant, then surveyed the beautifully ploughed field, and said sadly, 'Y'know what I'm going' till tell ye. I'm mortal glad ye did what ye done before ye done what ye did.'

Again it was a son of the soil who astonished a visiting American he was showing round his farm. They came to a hedge laden with blackberries and the visitor asked, 'What kind of berries are those?'

'They're blackberries,' he was told. 'They're very popular in these parts.'

'But,' said the American, pointing at several unripe clusters, 'Surely those ones are red?'

'Of course,' said the farmer patiently, 'that's the cololur they are when they're green.'

The visitor is often taken to be unusually retarded, if not downright thick, when failure to 'understand English' is evident. If, for example, he doesn't appreciate that if advised he is 'No goat's toe' it signifies he has his wits about him.

And to the native it smacks of utter stupidity if, when you're told to 'pull the door after you', you look on it as an invitation to not just to close it but to drag it off its hinges and take it with you.

I was up at your house last night but you weren't in. Were you out?

When it comes to urban refinements of the vernacular as distinct from the rural variety, the line of demarcation has subtleties of its own in Ulster.

'I'll take a wee skite over till see you' is the way a townswoman would put it, while the statement 'The wee lad got his mutton dummies all wet' is rarely heard in the country as plimsolls are largely worn by town youngsters. They would not be considered sufficiently stout footwear around a farm.

A man was knocked down by a car at a city crossroads and a group of the curious gathered round his unconscious figure as the ambulance was awaited.

A passer-by joined the group and inquired of the person nearest, 'Has he been hurt?'

'We don't rightly know,' came the cautious answer. 'He hasn't spoken yet.'

In the country the reply would probably have run, 'Mind ye I wudn't think he'll be diggin' any potatoes for a day or two.'

No countrywoman would tell a friend, 'I was up at your house last night but you weren't in. Were you out?' In rural areas people don't drop in without warning to the same extent as in the town.

And it is highly unlikely that this exchange would take place other than between two townspeople:

'You're drippin' so ye are. Was it wet?'

'Aye but it wasn't much. Just big gaps.'

The kind of statement apt to be heard in the town is 'If you're goin' to stand out there you'd better come in an' close the door.' In the country callers don't normally linger hesitantly on the doorstep.

A countryman would complain 'They never ast me had had I a mouth on me'. On the other hand a townsman would usually say outright 'Wud ye like a wee rosiner?' and that would be that.

Another way of saying 'Don't bother going to the trouble' runs 'Don't bother your Barney.' It is not now heard so frequently.

The suggestion was made to me that the phrase had its origin in the fact that the Barney originally referred to was a donkey.

I am convinced that it was a townswoman who sought to voice her indignation that the bus she boarded went by a different route so that shown on the indicator sign.

'It isn't right,' she protested angrily. 'It shudda went the way it was wrote.'

It is not easy to work out what precisely was meant by the statement 'That fella has a funny laugh.' More easily understood is the complaint 'I was done to my face.'

And there is a townswoman's enthusiasm about the tribute, 'Your wee Jamsie's no dozer. I knew he had a head on him the minnit I clapped eyes on him.'

Emphasising the distinction between town and country is the reply of an applicant for a job with a light engineering firm in Belfast, asked what his previous occupation had been:

'I humphed stuff about most of the time but I tuk a bad back out of it an' the tablets the doctor giv' me did me no good. I get red of it myself so I did, doin' exercises our Sammy showed me.'

No countryman would be guilty of such frankness.

But townsfolk have their own idiosyncrasies in other respects.

They'll say, for example, 'We're goin' go have wor tea,' or 'We'll take wor time.' In this respect they display an odd similarity to the language of the Geordie whose 'Wordaz on the buroo', meaning 'father is out of work', has its own connotations with 'Worteez ready', which means in Ulster 'The tea is on the table.'

The lady who complained 'I was had' shared something in common with her neighbour who said 'I was dropped on.' In a different category was the woman who told a caller 'I didn't hear you knock the first time.' The caller, in fact, was the rent man.

Apt to confuse the stranger is 'I don't drink but I can pass myself.' It is another way of intimating 'I'm not a teetotaller but then neither would I be mortally offended if you offered me a drink.'

There is the mark of the sophisticated townswoman who said, 'Winnie wore them wedgies of hers for a whole fortnight before she put them on.'

And it is a safe bet that a town dweller was referred to in the statement 'He's away upstairs to get his head down for half an hour.' Farm folk don't normally go to bed for a short rest. Usually when they go they go for the night.

'Have you your smoothin' done?' is essentially a townswoman's query, as is 'Are you only after putten that dress on?'

In the matter of getting up in the morning early rising is basic to the life style of farm folk. In the town they show a leg with the greatest reluctance.

Once I was told of the astonishment of an English guest in a Belfast household because each morning the woman of the house would go to the foot of the stairs and call 'Yup?'

A moment or two later the reply would come 'Mup.'

In fact the same story is well known in Geordie country, the words unchanged.

It is also familiar in Yorkshire, where the version is a shade more elaborate. It takes this form:

'Yup?'
'Ibed.'
'Grup.'
'Shrup.'
'Grup.'
'Mup.'

'He hadn't a leg to stand on for the arms they found on him.'

Ulster's years of violence have made their own contribution to folk speech. Murders, assassinations, bombings, turmoil and turbulence have failed to dampen the people's instinct to bear up in the face of the worst.

Demonstrating this resolute doggedness with disaster all around is to hear it said of an arrested suspect, 'He hadn't a leg to stand on for the arms they found on him.'

Women especially refuse to be completely dismayed. 'The gowls of them saccharine tanks is terrible' somehow makes these menacing Saracens much less malevolent, reducing the panoply of soldiery to domestic proportions.

An Army patrol's arrival at the front door acquires a different dimension when it is said, 'The corpular has rapped with the butt of his rifle.'

And what could be more disarming than the description of a death-dealing weapon, 'He had one of them machine guns with the barrel all holes.'

The road ramp is a familiar Ulster device to discourage high speeds when wrongdoers are escaping. There are people, however, to whom they are unfamiliar.

This was the case when a Belfastwoman was homeward bound in one of the black taxis that are now a feature of the city's transport system. They are former London taxis and run like buses on the regular routes.

The taxi gave a jolt and the woman asked 'Did you hit something?'

'It's all right,' the driver replied. 'We've just gone over a ramp.'

'Did ye kill it?' she asked anxiously.

The same approach was displayed by a woman who felt a profound sympathy for an Army sentry involved in a long spell of duty inside a street corner post, well covered with strips of cotton camouflage.

'I felt that sorry for him,' she told a friend. 'I just went home and made him a wee apple tart and pushed it into the sowl through the dulse.'

To hear it said, 'Them sojers put ma windas in' calls for some thought before one can work out whether the windows had been smashed or, having been smashed, the thoughtful soldiery replaced them.

No translation is needed for the statement 'The Black Watch thoo an accordion roun' the block.'

The complaint 'I nivver closed my eyes all night with their boots' merely emphasised the noisiness of the well-shod Army patrols.

Nevertheless there are occasions when the Army's desire to be of help is not fully appreciated.

This happened when an old people's club came under fire from terrorist snipers. All the occupants were safely evacuated except for three aged men and a fleshless old lady playing a card game in a far corner of the building, their drinks beside them.

Eventually by creeping on his hands and knees, with bullets crashing through the windows above him at intervals, a sergeant managed to reach the quartet, who paid no attention to him.

Impatiently he tugged at the woman's skirt, saying urgently, 'Missus, I'm here to rescue you. Hurry up and come on.'

Unconcernedly she grasped her glass, turned, gave him a look of scorn, and said, 'Buzz aff, James Bond.'

Members of Her Majesty's Forces from other UK areas where standard English is spoken must encounter adjustment problems when they first arrive in Northern Ireland.

One of them might not unreasonably feel uneasy if he heard the man standing beside him in a chemist's ask 'Cud I have a bottle for throwing off?' After all he could well be a petrol bomber, out shopping.

The way the ladies have of putting things is constantly unusual. For instance the woman who remarked to a friend, 'Luck at that helicopter wi' its door lyin' open.' And the lady who watched a group of rioters being shepherded into a police van, 'D'ye see that? They have them handcuffed by the feet.'

'We usually have our tea about sex.'

The eccentricities that distinguish Ulster's use of the Queen's English are not confined to strictly grammatical deviations. A letter will be omitted from a word just as casually as one will be added, for no apparent reason.

Continually, for example, a reference to the Admiralty is turned into the 'Admirality.' The extra letter is taken for granted.

This tendency results in a wide-ranging list of persistent oddities, such as:

'We all went to the azoo.'

'We was indentified.'

'The wee lad's very athaletic.'

'I saw her at Christamas.'

'They all went intil the shop.'

'He's an MP at Westminister.'

'Buzz aff, James Bond.'

'You should have seen our Kathaleen.'
'A man needs an incentative.'
'He can make no hand of the mathametics.'
'The match was postponded.'
'It was a right good filum.'
'The wee girl's brother was drownded.'
'He's an Eytalian.'

The list of words deliberately shortened or otherwise distorted is no less extensive. For example,

We had a pumpture.'
'He had to go to the infirmry.'
'We were talking at the City Hall about the Lord Morality.'
'The fella was parletic.'
'We went to Robison and Cleaver's.'
'I'm going to the libery.'
'The match was defitely off.'
'The pesperation was running aff me.'

If the statement is made 'Her maiden name was Camel' what is actually being indicated is that the girl was formerly called Campbell.

The 'r' syndrome is extensive in its ramifications. It doesn't end with the transformation of mother into 'mor.'

If a woman shopper advises a companion 'We have till use the orr dure' her intention is to say that a different entrance is called for. Another set of circumstances is involved when you hear the words inside the store, 'I'm luckin' for the entrance out.'

If a reference to 'Norn Iron' is made it is an allusion to Northern Ireland geographically, not to its minerals.

A confession by a parent that he gave his boy 'a right larrn' means that the youngster was the recipient of 'a right leathering', another way of describing a good beating.

The statement 'He went and forgot to tare the horse' is an indication that someone was thoughtless enough to leave the animal untethered.

To be asked 'Isn't the ware terrible?' is not an effort to seek confirmation that something offered for sale is poor value. It means what it says — that the weather was awful.

The news that the flower show was 'abonded because it was spittin' implies that the day wasn't all that bad and that the speaker felt it should have gone on as usual.

Glentoran is a well-known Belfast soccer team but not even the most fervent supporter calls it by any other name than 'Glenturn.' It is the 'r' syndrome in a different form.

If you are told that someone is 'very thora' a compliment is being paid. The idea is to underline that he is whole-hearted in everything he does. If you give him a job he will do it.

On the other hand an Ulsterman who wants to make it known that he has tossed something aside, something of no further value, will say 'I thew it away.'

In the matter of figures the idiom has produced a whole series of complications.

Around Ballymena, where everyday speech sounds as Scottish as any part of Scotland, nobody would dream of saying 'One.' It's always 'yin', just as 'two' is turned into 'twa.'

Illustrating this propensity is the story of the visit by a Department of Education inspector to a primary school. He asked the class 'How many are one and one?' There was complete silence, even when he repeated the question.

Then the teacher stepped into the breach and asked 'How many are yin and yin?

'Twa' roared the class triumphantly.

The 'r' complication once more raises its head when we come to 'three.' The simple request 'three threes' becomes 'thee thees' in many parts of Ulster, and an article priced at three pence is transformed into an item costing 'thee p.'

When it comes to four the pronunciation usually takes the form 'fower.' This, in fact, is the Elizabethan spelling.

So too with five. A favourite variation in this case produces the statement 'I have an appointment on the fith of Febery.' Actually this isn't the only month apt to be distorted. A favourite habit is to turn April into Aprile.

A visit to Ballymena swiftly establishes the lengths to which the figure six can be taken. The best known variation produced there came in answer to a visiting social worker who asked 'What do you do about sex in this area?' Promptly came the answer 'We usually have our tea about sex.'

When people speak figuratively nine produces unusual results. It will often be pronounced 'niyen', sharply and incisively. There is no possibility of it being mistaken for anything else. It receives rather similar treatment to the word 'coort.' It is recognised that an Ulsterman is capable of putting more bite into the word when speaking of courting a girl than is the case in any other part of the country.

A further curiosity in Northern Ireland speech is past tense of the word 'divide', which produces 'They divid it between them.'

Another idiomatic abberation is the use of the expression 'awa' in conversation. This is because of a reluctance to resort to 'er' when there is

35

uncertainty over a word or a name.

You will be told 'I was talking the other day to awa. You know the man? Awa.' In other words the speaker can't remember his name.

But he would never dream of adding to the confusion of a stranger by talking in this fashion. The point is he knows that someone who speaks the language will understand him perfectly.

'Awa' pops up in other circumstances. A Belfast visitor was completely confused when a man in search of the C and A store said to him, 'Mister, cud ye tell me how till get till Seeanawa's.'

The origins for this oddity are as far distant as those to blame for such abortions of pronunication as 'biceleek' for bicycle, 'bastick' for basket, and 'bistick' for 'biscuit', 'bronical' for 'bronchial'.

In the matter of names people called Campbell aren't the only sufferers. Anyone whose name is Hugh is highly vulnerable.

A woman went into a Belfast store, a small boy by her side, and asked for a school blazer with the initial 'S' on the breast pocket.

The assistant made an examination of his stock and explained 'I'm terribly sorry, madam. I'm afraid we haven't any on the shelves just at the moment. If you could come back in a couple of weeks, perhaps?'

'That's too long to wait,' the woman said firmly. She grabbed the boy by the hand and added, 'Come on Shuey, we'll try somewhere else.'

Oddly enough, while the point of this story would be appreciated in most parts of Northern Ireland, across the border it would draw a blank.

The reason is that elsewhere in Ireland the woman would have asked for a blazer with 'Q' on it.

'Every time he opens his mouth he takes a wrong step.'

Folk in Ulster are rarely hesitant when assessing an acquaintance — whether liked or disliked.

'Whoever reared her would drown nothing.'

'Every time he opens his mouth he takes a wrong step.'

The lady who had 'a neck like a bottle of castor oil' did not necessarily have the same limitations as the woman who was 'very tall across,' while if it is said of you 'If you had a couple of holes in your back you'd make a light flute' carries the message that there's no need for you to go on a diet.

It is not intended as a testimonial to a hair stylist if it is said, 'She can be very cuttin'.' The implication is simply that 'she has a tongue,' otherwise 'a tongue that would clip tin.'

Subtleties of their own are hinted at in the pronouncements 'He has a heart of gold and a brass neck to go with it', and 'He's a big man but a wee coat fits him.'

Sometimes people's own admissions can reveal much more about them than the appraisals of others.

It is impossible not to visualise the sterling innocence of the woman who was describing her efforts to drown her aged cat. 'I was holding it down in a bucket of water when it sunk its teeth in my thumb. Imagine it doing that after me always being so good to it.'

Similarly a picture of the owner of a corner shop is immediately conjured up by the words, 'It was a great wee place. They sold everything. There was an empty jampot on the counter with a spoon inside it and a notice alongside saying "Rattle for attention."'

The man who was 'very fond of a jar' was by no means a total abstainer and the gentleman who was 'a great believer in porridge for his bowels' was clearly not one for neglecting his health.

'Oul head-the-ball' does not come within the category of a complimentary label, unlike 'He plays with the head,' which does. A choice insult is 'He's as good as a man short.' Exactly the opposite is indicated by 'He's very handy with his feet.' The youth whose father said he was 'futless with his left hand' is outside all classifications.

An element of disfavour is obvious in the judgement, 'You'd think she owned the town and yet she hasn't the nails to scratch herself with.'

In the same sisterhood is the woman of whom it was complained, 'When she opens the door you don't know if she'll have a face on her or not.' This conveys the message that a visit to her is an uncertain business. It all depends on her mood.

A fertile imagination is summed up in 'He always sees more nor what was there.' This also applies to 'You couldn't believe the opposite to what he says.'

A different set of character deficiencies is indicated in 'He has nó bowels of compassion.'

'In my days all the plastic shoes were made of leather' is a remark from someone who finds difficulty in moving with the times.

'If it's a day like that tomorrow I'll go out in my figure,' means that a decision not to wear a coat has been made. In Ulster it is the ultimate in respectability for a lady to be seen 'out in her figure.'

'He'd rise at midnight to oblige you' pays its own handsome tribute and there is a kindliness all its own about the description of a retarded boy 'He has a wee want in him.'

The secret of winning friends has obviously escaped the man summarised by 'If he was thrown after you, you wouldn't luck round to see what the clatter was.'

A similar lack of acceptability is shown by, 'He would clap you on the back before your face and cut your throat behind your back.'

It should be noted that a man who 'gets his hair cut religiously every fortnight' is more concerned with his appearance than the hereafter.

If you are told of someone 'I haven't a word to say against him' it is advisable to be on your guard. The truth of the matter is that the speaker is convinced that he is a liar and a cheat, a blackguard of the deepest dye, with a family background so unfortunate that it is impossible for him ever to overcome it.

Incidentally, this advice applies no less to the south than to the north in Ireland.

'That fella could talk for another row of teeth' is no sufferer from taciturnity, unlike someone of whom it is said in 'All he does is sit there scringing his dentures' or 'When he comes to the house he just sits there like a delph King William.'

Strictly in the ill-mannered class is the visitor in the indictment, 'When he comes to the house he only gants all night.' What is meant is that he yawns his head off, making no effort to conceal his boredom.

'I know her, the police know her but nobody decent knows her' puts into a nutshell someone with highly undesirable qualities, the kind which indices the reaction described by 'I saw her but I never looked at her.'

There is an ominousness of its own about 'He'll not last long for there's the smell of clay off him.' Equally foreboding is the reply given to a man who had spent some little time reciting the drawbacks of his ailment, 'Sure I knew a fella had exactly the same trouble as you, God rest him.'

A desire to express appropriate sympathy with a vocabulary limited in the extreme is revealed in the exchange,

'My brother-in-law dropped dead in the street, so he did. It was a terrible shock.'

'Did he now? That was ratten for him.'

Delicacy in the use of language is constantly encountered, especially in rural areas. It is difficult to picture a more lyrical farewell than, 'Well, you'll be off now but don't be sad for sure it will not be long till after a while and you'll be back again seeing me.'

It makes a fascinating exercise to picture the lack of bias of the soccer fan whose companion said at the turnstile, 'You should let Jimmy in for half price for he only sees the one team.'

And the old age pensioner had a conspicuously down to earth view of political promises when she was told that the Government intended to announce an increase in old age pensions in the April Budget. It was then December and she made a swift calculation of the time still to pass and said, 'Mind you a quare lot of us'll have had a slap in the face with a shovel before next April comes round.'

It is doubtful if the youth whose hair was 'as long as the 119th Psalm' would appreciate the point. Youths in this category aren't usually so steeped in Scriptural knowledge as to be aware that the Psalm has 176 verses.

'She let her cheese get too hard before she put it in the mousetrap.'

In matters of the heart Ulster has its own archetypal undertones. This is especially the case in farming districts. There are many rural areas that have yet to yield to today's concepts of love and marriage.

Illustrating the down-to-earth attitude consistently encountered is the reassuring comment of the bride-to-be whose prospective husband was highly conscious of his lack of good looks.

'You know, Mary,' he said, 'I'm surprised you had me at all, considering that I'm not what you could call an oil painting.'

'For goodness sake don't let that worry you,' she replied. 'Sure you'll be out at your work all day.'

The other side of the coin is shown by the answer of the bridegroom when asked at the wedding ceremony, 'Do you take this woman to be your lawful wedded wife?'

'Man dear, sure that's what I'm here for,' was the blunt reply.

There is an essentially Ulster flavour about the words of the Belfastwoman involved in a court application for maintenance.

She was asked what exactly had happened to her relationship with her husband and carefully explained, 'To tell you the truth there wasn't a thing wrong for the first five years. He was that nice to me we could have been strangers.'

Somewhat similar was the case of the nervous bridegroom who refused to accept his father's reassurances that in getting married he had really nothing to worry unduly about.

'It was all right for you,' came the protest. 'You married my ma. I'm marrying a stranger.'

Even after many years of marriage there is a dogged insistence on independence, as if togetherness meant losing something. It is not so long since this was demonstrated to a new minister who called to see a member of the congregation.

The man's wife answered the door and when the minister asked if the man of the house was at home he was told, 'Aye, William Chambers is in the house.' It was not 'Yes, my husband is at home.' The statement was made as if it was a perfectly natural way of referring to her spouse. It was not meant in the least offensively.

It isn't always advisable to be over-enthusiastic about a lady's choice. There is a characteristic touch about the retort of a young woman when told, 'That's a right steady young fellow you're going about with.'

'Aye,' she answered, 'and if he was any steadier he'd be motionless.'

Appearances, however, can often count.

A great deal of talk followed when a widow, rather tall in stature, suddenly married again. Her choice as a partner was considerably shorter than she was.

This inspired the comment from one of her neighbours, 'Mind you, a quare lot of her's going to sleep alone at night.'

Height was also an element in a country match which fell through. The prospective bridegroom wryly explained to a friend, 'Ach she was far too tall for me. I'm over six fut but sure if I was standing beside her she cud bake pancakes on my head.'

No less realistic was the response when one of the town's bachelors announced his intention to marry and was told of the intended bride, 'But she's a bit plain, isn't she?'

'Plain,' was his response. 'Sure they're all the same from the chin down.'

Forthrightness is similarly evident in the allusion to the woman who had set her cap at one of the town males at a period considered to be rather late in her life, 'All that's wrong with her is that she let her cheese get too hard before she put it in the mousetrap.'

Another way of indicating that the boat has been missed is to say, 'Sure the sun's aff her winda long ago.'

The confession 'I took my dead end at him' implies that the gentleman made a good impression.

But proposals of marriage don't come easily to the Ulsterman. It means taking a fateful step, something that calls for careful thought. Even when the vital question is finally put there is a cautiousness about the wording.

An example is the farmer who invited the lady of his choice to the house and, as the evening was almost at its end and she was thinking of leaving, he exclaimed, 'Minnie, will you sit there for good?'

Male caution, naturally, can occasionally lead to unexpected expressions of feminine impatience. One thwarted Co Antrim girl put it like this to a young admirer, unduly wary about getting his feelings into words: 'If you're goin' till tak us tak us, if you're not goin' till tak us tell us.'

Trying to take the bull by the horns, however, can have unexpected results.

One young woman was discussing with a friend the persistent reluctance shown by an admirer of long standing. She was advised that he needed a push or nothing would ever happen. 'Tell him you have decided to go to America,' she was told. 'If there's anything that'll put a match to him that will.'

That evening she dropped her bombshell. The news was greeted with several moments of silence, then he turned to her and said, 'D'ye know this? It's the best thing you've ever done.'

'Him and her's thick' is not a comment intended to imply that a couple aren't particularly bright, rather that they are 'going steadily together,' nothing more.

Just as there is a distinct flavour of envy about the retailing of the news of an engagement, 'She's marrying in a month or two. They say he's a prosperous wee man with three cows and a horse and cart all giving milk.'

It isn't easy to give any further emphasis to the mordant comment about one gentleman who finally named the day, 'It was about time he married her. Sure he had the shoes walked aff her.'

The relationship of the sexes is particularly highlighted by the conversation between two old friends, John and Robert James. John's wife had just died and Robert James called to offer his condolences. They sat gazing into the fire as they talked.

'She was the right wee woman, John.'

'Aye, she was that.'

'She was the gran' cook.'

'She wasn't bad at the cookin' at all.'

'You'll quarely miss her, mind you.'

'Aye, I will that.'

'How long were you married, John? It was a long time.'

'I was more nor fifty years married to her and do you know what I'm goin' till tell you, Robert James? I nivver liked her.'

No less dogged was the attitude reflected by the reluctant wooer who had finally named the day. On the eve of the wedding he called on the bride to be and said, 'Ah was just wonderin' there if ye had any noting of rueing.

For if ye hev it doesn't make wan bit of odds.'

Again, there was the case of the man who had been courting steadily for years, seeing the loved one with unfailing regularity twice a week. Eventually a friend asked him if he didn't think it was time he got married and settled down.

'What,' was the reply, 'and have nowhere to go every Tuesday and Thursday.'

'She's that good she bites the altar rails.'

There are few more fruitful sources for a student of the vernacular than an Ulster bus. It can be highly stimulating to sit behind two chatting women, or two men engaged in active discussion. The air can be filled with such gems of expression as:

'That fella misses nathin'. He cud hear a feather fallin' in cotton wool.'

'She's awful religious got. She's that good now she bites the altar rails.'

'I told him straight — whatever you say, say nothing.'

'D'ye mind the day it snowed? I told the milkman he had his wellies on the wrong feet and he said "But they're the only feet I've got." '

Many people seem to look on a bus as a kind of confessional. They'll use it for making the most intimate revelations without turning a hair. For example:

'I'll say this about him. He has no right to complain about discrimination. He has nine children and not a Protestant among them.'

'When our Bella's sleepin' her big eyes are like bin lids.'

'That fella Mary Jane's goin' about with. Sure he can't read or write. He doesn't know a T from the head of a crutch.'

It was an obviously married couple who were involved in one unusual exchange. She was formidable; he was small and clearly very much under her thumb. He had just finished a meticulous search of his pockets.

'Do you know what I have got?' he asked in a timid voice.

'What have you got?' was the impatient reply.

'I have got my gloves lost.'

Two parcel-laden women on their way home from a shopping expedition were talking and one said, 'I thought yousens had a wee car. D'ye not go in it?'

42

'A bit big for his age, isn't he?'

'Wud ye have sense?' came the answer. 'By the time ye'd get a place till park it I cud have the clothes bought and wore out.'

A ticket collector was making one of his random checks. He was small but resolute and firmly confronted a woman accompanied by a youth for whom she had produced a child's ticket.

The inspector regarded him suspiciously and said, 'A bit big for his age isn't he?'

'Aye he is,' the mother answered, 'an' that's more than ivver yir mother cud say about you.'

There is a fireside intimacy about the dialogue between two corpulent ladies, quite unconcerned whether anyone was listening or not.

'How's yir Ant Lizzie these days?'

'Ach she's not too gran' at all.'

'What ails her then?'

'Ach she's got her bad leg back again.'

'I'm quare an' sorry to hear the like so I am.'

'Aye, she's had it on and off for the past wheen o' months but like many's another body she just has to thole it when she has it.'

It often happens that a story circulating in one community and thought to have originated there is familiar to another. Pinpointing story sources with precision is nearly impossible.

I wouldn't doubt for a moment that Glasgow, Manchester, Birmingham or Cardiff could just as readily be the source of the following exchange as Belfast, where I am assured it actually was heard.

A woman asked a bus driver if his vehicle would be sure to take her past a particular hospital.

'It won't missus,' she was told. 'If you get the next one coming you'll be all right.'

'But will the next bus be long,' she demanded impatiently.

'Missus,' he said, 'it'll be the same length as this one.'

'And will it have a monkey on it as well?' she called out as he pulled away.

The well-being of friends is a constant source of comment, whether the bus is empty or full.

'She looks all right now but she was mortal bad last week.'

'She was all failed. If I was her I'd go down till the morgue and wait till I was identified.'

All kinds of treasure trove can come the way of those who keep an ear cocked between the stops:

'Ye just can't bate two farls of fadge fried with an egg.'

'There's this about that wee woman. If she's ast till a weddin' she'd nearly stay for the christenin'.'

'Them weans of hers, sure their noses are always trippin' them.'

'She has a neb on her like a ferret.'

On a bus packed to suffocation the conductor kept pleading with the passengers, 'Move up everybody. Ye'll have to move up.'

'Ach,' came a hoarse voice from somewhere at the back. 'If I move up any more I'll get run over.'

A passenger who boarded a bus heading out of Ballymena had his wife and child with him. He told the conductor, 'an inses an' an outses for her and me an' itses.' In other words he wanted three return tickets.

Occasional slight difficulties of communication naturally arise, as in this piece of dialogue between two men:

'He was stannin' there rightly all night.'

'He was what?'

'He was bloody rightly.'

'You mean he was stovin'?'

'Isn't that what I just told you. He was rightly.'

One passenger was heard to confide to his companion, 'The toe's out of the heel of my sock so it is.' For no apparent reason this inspired the reply, 'Sure in this place if it's not rainin' it's pourin'.'

And there was a note of profound wonderment about the way an elderly passenger confided to the woman beside him, 'The two wee lads were playing at the back. One of them skint his knee and started wailing that his leg was broke. Wee Alec takes a look at it and says "Sure it's only bleedin'. It's better bleedin' nor beelin'." He's an oul fashioned wee thing, Alec. That wee lad was here before, I said.'

Nor does 'here before' imply that he had paid an earlier visit. The suggestion is that he had been on earth before.

'He's a quare hand with a spade but he's a quare oul pahle.'

Ulster shares many idiomatic idiosyncrasies with the rest of Ireland, just as they are shared with Scotland. Gaelic usages figure almost as extensively in everyday Belfast speech as is the case in Dublin. For example, North and South have the same tendency to apply the word 'quare' to almost everything under the sun.

I am not sure, however, that if an Ulsterman called someone 'a quare fellow' it would have the same meaning as that implicit in Brendan Behan's *The Quare Fellow*. In Northern Ireland the word can be used to mean exceptional, wonderful, curious, odd, peculiar, fantastic, abnormal, unique. The individual concerned can have any, or all, maybe even none of these qualities.

Ulster people will say 'She's a quare nice wee girl' or 'She's quare and thran', which means the opposite. A boy can be 'quare and smart' or 'quare and cheeky.' It can be 'a quare wet day' or 'a quare nice day.' An article can be 'quare and dear' or 'quare and cheap'.

A man can be 'a quare hand with a spade' or 'a quare oul pahle'. If you have 'a quare eye in your head' the implication is that you don't miss much.

'Brave' is another portmanteau word, used as Shakespeare used it.

A morning can be 'brave and warm' or 'brave and cold'. A meal can be 'brave and good', a gathering 'brave and big'. You can be 'feeling bravely' after an illness.

'A brave wee woman' can be six feet tall and not particularly heroic. 'A brave wee soul' can be a child who makes a good impression.

By any reckoning that's a brave selection.

If a reference is made to 'suchina day' this has different connotations to those involved in calling it 'brave'. The word implies that the weather conditions are terrible, certainly unusually unpleasant.

Another word with an infinity of uses is 'on'. This is a tendency which produces statements like

'He ate my sweets on me.'

'He shut the door on me.'

'Have you a £1 on you?'

'He told on me.'

'My tie fell on me.'

'She's married on a cousin of mine.'

'He lost it on me.'

46

It can also produce the complaint 'I asked her not to let on', implying that a confidence was completely misplaced.

In Ulster anyone who is 'dead bate' is really exhausted. If he is 'dead done' he is in much the same condition. There are other refinements of the word.

A Co Antrim workman was engaged in road alterations at Belfast Airport and a distinguished physicist, taking a walk while awaiting his plane, stopped to watch him.

The work involved lining up some piping and the physicist said, 'You have to be pretty accurate lining that up, haven't you?'

'Aye. Right enough,' said the workman.

'Actually in my own laboratory the need for precise accuracy is of tremendous importance. In my own case if I'm ten-thousandths of an inch out in my calculations the result could be downright disaster.'

'Cud it?' said the workman. 'But that wouldn't do us, mister. We havta be dead on.'

Many things treated elsewhere as being singular are considered to be plural in Ulster.

For example, 'them' rather than 'it' is applied to porridge. The same applies to stew. It is not unusual for the comment to be heard after a bowl of broth is consumed, 'Man they were good.'

Confusion over the exact occasions on which 'to' should properly be used rather than 'till' can bring complications. This was demonstrated by a piece of dialogue at a Belfast bus terminal.

'Could you tell me when this bus leaves?'

'Ten till.'

'Ten till? You're sure it isn't ten past?'

'It used to be ten past but it has been ten till for a good while now.'

'The last time I caught it, it went at ten to.'

'No, it's ten past. It was ten to for a while there, then they changed it to ten till.'

The conversation would be apt to leave a stranger convinced that the two people were talking in some kind of code rather than in standard English.

I have already quoted examples of Ballymena speech. I might add to them the case of the English motorist who found himself there after touring the rest of Ireland. He noticed that the conventional British colour of the pillar boxes contrasted with those in the South, where they are painted green.

'I see the pillar boxes are red here,' he commented to a native.

'They are indeed,' was the reply. 'They're red twice a day.'

A few miles from the town it would not be unusual to hear a farmer giving utterance to this piece of agricultural wisdom, 'If you henna any hey in by the end of July ye'll nae hev any hey at all.'

And it was at a Co Antrim goods depot that a telephone call was received asking if a mare could be collected that afternoon for delivery to another townland. The arrangements were duly completed and a horse box lined up and despatched on tow to make the collection.

An hour or so later car and horse box returned to the depot. No animal was to be seen and the driver was asked what had gone wrong.

'There's your mare,' he said gloomily and produced a small bathroom mirror.

Complications constantly arise when words are taken at their face value.

To be informed 'I have just bought an oul coat' means that the purchase of a brand new garment has been completed. A baby can be 'an oul darling', and a ruffian 'an oul rogue'.

If the complaint is made 'the oul rheumatism's at me' it can be assumed, however, that it has struck before.

'Before you go to bed don't forget to lose your laces.'

The small boy whose mother rebuked him with the words, 'You went and tore your bit of a good coat' may not have been aware that her English wasn't all that it should be; nevertheless he got the message.

He could well have been a younger brother of the lad who was said to be 'Bluemoulded for the want of a good hiding,' as neat a way as could be devised for indicating that he wasn't particularly well brought up. But then, who is to say?

Certainly from an early age the Ulster child has his ears assailed with English at its oddest. How many hairdressers outside Northern Ireland would understand the parental instruction when a small boy is delivered into their hands, 'Slipe it brave and close for it's a harbour for vermin.'

It is only a small step for the same child to tell his friends, 'We didn't half go coming back.'

In the same singular vein is the maternal injunction, 'Before you go to bed don't forget to lose your laces.'

The trials of an Ulster teacher are doubtless no worse than those in any other community but more often, at least, they have their amusing side.

48

I like to think that it was an Ulster youngster, and not one from somewhere else, who went home in tears after his first day at school. He was asked why all the crying and said, 'Well, when I went into the classroom the teacher pointed to a chair and told me to sit there for the present I sat there till the bell went and never the present did I get.'

The world of childhood can have its harsher moments. It is easy to imagine the feelings of the small boy with rather large ears on hearing his mother confide to a visitor, 'Them lugs of his is that big we didn't know whether he would fly or walk when he was born.'

Still the fact is that children can bring their own sense of realism to matters, as happened when a youngster was taken visiting to family friends. They were noted for their hospitality and as the woman of the house began preparing a meal for the occasion her husband said, 'When you're at it put the child on an egg.'

The child instantly started wailing. 'I'm not going to sit on an egg for anybody', she protested.

It was a Co Down boy on his first day at the seaside who wanted to draw attention to the distance from the shore of some older members of the family out in a rowing boat.

'Look at the far out them'uns is went,' he cried.

The same sense of precision is evident in the case of the boy who was told, 'If you take pains with your homework you'll get a real reward.'

'But I'd rather not get any pains,' he replied.

A motorist was parking his car, conscious that he was not particularly expert at it. Cautiously he considered the available space, far from lavish. He saw a boy passing along the pavement and, hoping for some help, called out, 'Sonny, would you watch me while I park?'

'Why, are you good at it?' exclaimed the boy.

I have to confess to some difficulty in picturing the youngster of whom a fond relative said, 'Ach but hasn't he the right wee face for a minister?'

The same trouble arises when the statement is made, 'That wee lad is more like his brother than his brother is like himself.'

'I want a hat for a girl with a 32in bust.'

Shops, whether large or small, are a rich treasure-house for anyone who goes Ulsterism spotting. To the men and women behind the counters of Northern Ireland the upside down, teetering speech is a basic part of their life style; it perpetually assails them. There is no escape from it.

It could only have been in a country grocery store where a visitor listened in astonishment as he heard the order being given, 'I want a clarter of tea, a clarter of sugar, a clarter of resins, and a clarter of cream of clarter.'

A speech deficiency was a drawback when an applicant for a job as assistant was being interviewed in another grocery. It was thought he should be given a chance when he promised eagerly to be most careful about everything he said.

When his first customer arrived he explained that he was new to the job but assured the lady that he would do his best to give her every satisfaction, adding that he was studying the pronunciation of words very carefully.

'I can see you have your mind made up to get on,' she acknowledged, impressed. 'Just what are your reasons now?'

'Thirty p. a pound, sultanas 33p,' he promptly replied.

He was no less eager when attending to the wants of a later shopper who was buying the ingredients for a cake.

As he measured out the last item he said, 'My ma always told me that that sort of a cake is no good unless there's a wee knowin of brandy in it.'

'And how much is a wee knowin?' he was asked.

'Sure it's just what you'd know,' he replied.

No better lesson in the refinements of the idiom could have been given.

Handling what appear to be confusing moments is second nature to Ulster shopkeepers. When a small boy dashed in to one store, thrust a 50p piece in front of the assistant, and announced 'My ma wants you to break that', a visitor waited curiously to see if a hammer would be produced for the purpose.

Sizes are a constant source of difficulty. So often this essential piece of information has to be dragged out of the customer, almost by force.

A woman buying a carpet was asked the size of the room for which it was wanted. She thought carefully for a moment, then said helpfully, 'Well it takes six rolls to paper it.'

In a shoe shop a young man said he wanted to buy a pair for his aunt. They were to be a present. The colour, he said, didn't matter.

'What size?' he was asked.

'But I don't know the size.'

The assistant, doubtless reflecting 'Here's another Charley', shook his head in some despair and was spotted by the manager, who came over to help.

'What age is your aunt? he asked the young man. 'That might be a guide for us.'

The young man looked thoughtful, then said, 'Well, if she lives till the 23rd of October she'll be 84.'

Another woman shopper was unusually forthcoming when on a similar quest. On being asked the size she answered blandly, 'Well I take sixes but I find sevens so comfortable to tell you the God's truth I wear eights.'

A woman buying a window blind also had her answer pat when asked what size of window it was wanted for, 'It's twice the width of my handbag and a wee bit more.'

A shopper buying an article of clothing as a gift for a relation, was asked 'Is she tall or short?'

'I couldn't rightly say,' she answered. 'Any time I've seen her she's been sitting.'

There was a neat acknowledgement of the need for precision, however, in the reply of a woman in buying wool to knit a jumper. She was asked what colour she wanted.

'It's to match my sister's new skirt,' she explained. 'I want it the colour of a Marie biscuit dipped in tea.'

A new assistant in a Co Down store was asked in the course of his first morning (a) for a pair of 'Palishin' shoes', meaning leather ones as distinct from suede, and (b) for a pair of shoes with bacon-rind soles, otherwise crepe. He had to ruefully admit that, after all, there is a certain resemblance.

A Co Armagh man left a pair of shoes to be mended, and called a week later inquiring 'Are they done?'

'Done?' was the reply. 'Them shoes were done when you brought them.'

The unexpected request is always round the corner for Ulster's traders.

It can range from 'I'm lookin' for a pair of trouser clips for the bicycle' to 'Could I have a pair of trousers for the car?'

'Do you sell long-sleeved underpants?' is the kind of request the experienced shop assistant will take in her stride. This also applies to 'Would you have any half-inch metric bolts?' or 'I want a hat for a girl with a 32in bust.'

But the embarrassment of a new assistant can be readily pictured when approached by a mild little lady and asked in a small voice, 'Could you please tell me where I go to get felt?'

It clearly calls for a degree of local understanding to appreciate what is meant when a customer is asked, 'Is there any ham on your mind this morning?'

A shopper who obviously spoke the language was heard inquiring, 'Could I have three slices of belly bacon and would you cut it with the ham knife to flavour it?'

Whether vague or specific, the customer is always right in Ulster, or nearly always. It isn't only the shoppers uncertain of the size they want who can cause headaches.

A salesman in a carpet store had his patience sorely tried by a woman who was being extremely fussy about both colour and pattern. Each new roll she wanted hauled out for inspection increased his perspiration.

Finally when he was near complete exhaustion, and had spread out what was at least roll No. 20, she said, 'Ach, I don't think I'll bother after all. It was only a piece to stand the teapot on I was after anyway.'

'He was sent home from school because he was walking.'

Ulstermen abroad can easily find themselves in situations where a blank stare is produced when they open their mouths. A Belfastman on his first day in a Canadian works canteen was asked 'Would you like some coffee?'

'I'll have a wee taste,' he replied and could not understand why the waitress looked confused.

Perplexity again arose when a couple from Northern Ireland were giving their orders in an English cafe.

'We'll have tea and we'd both like fries,' the waitress was told.

The girl duly brought them tea and two bars of Fry's chocolate, no doubt writing her customers off as eccentrics.

The late Denis Ireland once told me of an encounter during his travels abroad which illustrates how pleasure at a meeting can span the globe.

He went into a well-known international bar in Shanghai where all races, colours and creeds were represented, and the drink available was no less varied. Spotting two British sailors, he made a fair guess that they would at least speak English, and spoke to one of them.

On being answered in a fine Belfast accent he revealed that he also came from there.

'Holy skin,' exclaimed the sailor, turning to call his comrade over. 'Hi Jimmy, here's a fella from the satty.'

If anyone in the place was listening they would hardly have understood, which would not have been the case at home where everyone speaks the language.

Nothing could be more explicit than the statement 'I'll make you a cup of tea when I come till myself,' or 'I was going to make you a wee cup of tea only the teapot ran out on me.'

'The language' covers a wide range of utterance. It covers such confidences as this, heard in a shopping queue, 'I went up to see Mrs Thingimabob. What's her name? You know the one that's married on the fella at the head of the road? Ach what d'ye call him? He's always hokin' in the garden. His name's on the tip of my tongue. Anyway, what d'ye know but they both had their arms tied up. One of them had given it a bad sprain but the other poor cratur was worse. She had it broke and that's twice as bad, seein' it was broke in two places. With God's help they'll pull through. You wouldn't like to see nathin' happen to them, wud ye? God forbid.'

She sounded exactly like the lady who told a friend of the experience of a neighbour's small son. She confided, 'He was sent home from school because he was walking.'

To an alien ear this would be as incomprehensible as the comment by a woman to a stranger she approached in a busy Belfast street, 'D'ye mind if I cross the road with you? I don't mind being hit by a bus so long as I'm not by myself.'

There is the same air of contradiction about the statement 'They don't speak.' It is quite erroneous to get the impression that two mutes are referred to.

Anyone to whom the greeting 'Bully oul Billy' is meaningless is missing a great deal. It is one way of saying 'How are you? Where on earth have you been? I'm glad to see you're looking well.'

A difficulty can also arise if one's word-power doesn't cover the advice given to a motorist unable to start his car because of a jammed starter pinion, 'Why don't you shuggly shoe it?'

It helps, too, if it is appreciated that the expression 'Quare man yir da' is an expression of disbelief, another way of saying 'How're ye Burke?' Both emphatically imply 'I don't believe a word you're saying.'

Spontaneous expressions of delight, on the other hand, can take unusual forms.

One woman, leaving a house after a particularly happy visit, plus an excellent meal, said to her hostess, 'Ach I wish I was only comin'.'

Overjoyed because her son had secured a Christmas job as a temporary postman a Belfast mother told a friend, 'It's great. It'll keep him from walking the streets so it will.'

Doubtless it was the same speaker, in a reference to her ailing husband, who said, 'Ach he'll be all right when he's a bit better.'

There is no evidence to establish whether or not the lady was 'called for her mother.' which is just another example of Ulster quaintness. 'Called for' is regularly used in preference to 'called after'.

Questioning the obvious is another striking idiosyncrasy.

Anyone passing along the street, using a walking stick and obviously suffering from a foot injury of some kind, will take it as perfectly natural to have the inquiry put to them, 'Are you limping?'

Similarly the possession of a magnificent summer tan, probably acquired at no little cost on the Continent, will inspire the query, 'Are you back from your holidays?'

A husband arriving home on a wet night, soaked to the skin, is almost certain to be greeted with the question, 'Is it raining?' and think nothing of it.

So too can run the welcome given to a guest invited for the evening. 'Have you arrived? they will be asked in all seriousness.

When going visiting in Ulster it is advisable to listen carefully. The advice 'Take off your coat and you'll feel the good of it going out' is an expression of hospitality at its most sincere. It means 'You're more than welcome. We're delighted you came. We hope you'll stay a while.'

There are circumstances, though, when warmth should not be taken for granted. 'I see you're back' is a statement that can occasionally bring the sharp response 'Why what's wrong with it?'

This is not unlike the reply made by a laggard workman who was told by his overseer 'You should have been here at eight.'

'Why, what happened?' he retorted.

Rather in the same spirit was the reply given to a man who dashed into the office of a Belfast estate agent and asked 'Can I use your phone?'

'How do I know,' came the brusque answer. 'Have you ever used a telephone before?'

But it is fairly certain that it was an Ulster mother, watching her daughter washing the dishes, who called out as she saw a plate placed perilously near the edge of a shelf, 'Mary, set that up straight for I can see its ghost on the flure.'

It was a distinctly raw beginner in a Belfast office who answered the telephone with the inquiry, 'Was yous ones wantin' us ones for wir bell was ringing.'

Certainly those not privy to the patois face quite unexpected pitfalls. A woman visitor started up a conversation with a Co Down farmhand. He complained that he was very tired.

'Is that so?' she asked sympathetically. 'The work is hard?'

'My back's nearly broke,' he answered. 'I've been rapin' in that field there for the last three hours.'

She gave him a look of horror and took to her heels.

'He's our man. Sure you could feel the spits of him five pews away.'

Clerical involvement is inevitable where Ulster speech is concerned. The church has a close association with the day to day lives of the people. It follows that the pastoral story is part and parcel of the idiom.

It is, perhaps, not always easy to tell how many of them vary from stories relating to clerics in other communities. The dialect is different.

In one Ulster congregation it was the custom to invite a distinguished divine for an annual special service. When this happened the wife of one of the leading members, noted for her cookery, usually had the task of preparing a special spread for the visitor.

This time she had excelled herself. The table groaned with her efforts, only for her to be told by the visitor that he was very sorry but he always found that he spoke much more effectively on an empty stomach. To her mortification all he had was a glass of milk and a biscuit.

She herself did not attend the service but afterwards she asked her husband, 'Well, how did he do?'

'To tell you the truth,' was the answer, 'he might as well have ate his fill.'

A big occasion in a country congregation is the trial run of a prospective new minister. The debate afterwards to decide whether or not he is the man for the job is sometimes acrimonious.

For once the issue did not seem to be in doubt, at least according to one prominent member of the congregation.

'He's our man,' he said firmly. 'Sure you could feel the spits of him five pews away.'

Disenchantment, however, can eventually set in. It could well have been the same cleric at whose manse fire broke out. The firemen were heard to have voiced grave concern in case the flames reached his study.

'You could feel the spits of him five pews away.

'If it gets there the manse is done for,' one said. 'That's where he keeps his sermons and they're that dry the place will go up like tinder.'

Harvest services have a strong attraction. One ardent supporter of these occasions was heard to tell a friend she hadn't been able to get to as many as usual because of the drain of the collections on her resources.

'But why do you let that worry you?' she was challenged. 'Sure I've done five of them so far on only 10p.'

Serving an apprenticeship as a country pastor has its uneasy moments. One young minister had the fright of his life when visiting one of his congregation for the first time. Often in Ulster country houses the front door is used only on rare occasions, everyday callers going in by the back. This often results in stiff front door locks because of the lack of use and frequently a hammer or a hatchet is kept handy to help ease the problem of opening the front door. When the minister called, knocked, and stood waiting at the front door, his astonishment can be imagined when he heard a voice call out hoarsely, 'Minnie get the hatchet. The new minister's called.'

Another pastor, this time of rather longer experience, did not turn a hair when visiting a farmer. As the visit neared its end he suggested the conventional moment or two of prayer, and noticed that the gardener working away outside was also a member of his congregation.

'Call him in and he can join us,' he told the farmer.

The farmer went over to the window, knocked on the pane and signalled to the gardener to come it, then returned smiling to his chair.

'You're smiling?' the minister said. 'What's amusing you?'

'It's just Robert William there,' was the answer. 'He thinks he's being called in for his tea. He's going to get the quare gunk.'

When it comes to upside-down tributes the Ulsterman is in a class of his own.

One cleric, leaving to take up a post in another parish, was receiving a farewell gift. The speaker handing it over said gravely, 'We're going to miss you. When you came here we didn't know what you were going to be like but sure didn't you turn out to be a big ignorant fella like the rest of us.'

Doubtless it was the same speaker who prefaced a farewell presentation on another occasion by saying 'We decided to give you a wee momentum.'

In the matter of music criticism the standards can at times be severe.

A woman soloist of some note had been the star attraction at a church concert and a farming member of the audience was asked afterwards what he thought of her.

'I'll say this,' he answered 'It took a right lot more outa her to sing that bit of a verse than it took me to fork the corn on top of them high stacks of mine.'

'I want to buy a wheen o' thon thrupenny stamps afore the prices are riz'.'

'They all went to the pictures barn me.'

This glossary, embracing words that are likely to leave the uninitiated confused, is designed strictly for Ulsterese beginners. It includes many of my own favourite examples of Ulster speech and usage, many of them referred to in the preceding pages. It is not intended to be in any way comprehensive. A much more definitive Ulster dialect dictionary is now being prepared by Professor J. Braidwood, Head of the Department of English Language and Literature, Queen's University.

ASSAY	Calling attention, as in 'Hi,' or 'Excuse me a moment.'
AUGHT	Any, as in 'They're finished. I henna aught left.'
BAKE	Face: 'He always has his bake buried in the paper.'
BARN	Excepting: 'They all went to the pictures barn me.'
BEELIN'	Suppurating, festering: 'My finger is beelin'.'
BISTICK	Cream cracker, ginger snap; any variety of biscuit.
BISILEEK	Bicycle
BORR	Bother: 'Nivver borr your head.'
BOW FADDLE	A violin in Ballymena.
BRAVE	Commendable, worthy, acceptable: 'She's a brave wee sort of a woman.'
BRAVELY	Doing well, could be worse: 'The wife's bravely so she is.'
BROR	A man with a sister; member of an Order.
BROW	Borrow, obtain a loan.
CHIMLEY	Place where soot is found.
CLEVER	Neat, tight-fitting, usually in reference to a garment.
COLLOGUE	Gossip, exchange confidences.
COG	Copy, imitate, crib.
COUL	Chilly, wintry.
COWLRIFE	Constantly shivering, highly conscious of the temperature.
CRACK	Lively chat.
CRIG	Injure a toe while walking, trip on the pavement.
CURNS	Currants.
CUT	Mortified, hurt, insulted.

59

DEAD END	Taken when a person is amused: 'I took my dead end at him.'
DINGE	Dent; mark with a surface impression.
DIP	Bread fried in the pan: 'My man's dyin' about dip.'
DUCLE	Rural term for a cockerel with no fighting instincts
DUKE	See juke.
DULSE	Edible seaweed.
DUNT	Knock, blow.
DURBLEY	Feeble, infirm, ailing.
EE-IT	Eight.
EKKER	Exercise, a pupil's homework.
FADGE	Potato bread, popular delicacy when fried.
FARR	Male parent
FERN	Foreign, alien.
FOG FEED	Lavish meal.
FUNKY KNUCKLES	Someone who uses his nails rather than his knuckles when playing marbles.
GALLUSES	Braces, substitute for a belt. Not to be confused with galoshes.
GEG	Comic, amusing person.
GENSEY	Jersey, jumper
GIRN	Cry, weep
GLEED	Low light
GUB	Face: 'I hit him in the gub.'
GUESS	What many Ulster people cook with
GULDER	Shout, roar loudly
GUNK	Disappointed: 'I felt awful gunked.'
HAPPED	Tucked in
HARRISHED	Aggravated, annoyed
HENNA	Have not. (see aught)
HERR	Polite term for human thatch: 'I'm getting my herr done.'
HINCH	Hip
IRON	Emerald Isle.
JAWBOX	Sink; place for washing dishes.
JUKED	Peek, peer, elude: 'He juked his head round the door.' 'He's a quare hand at jukin' the peelers.' (see duke)
KYART	Vehicle drawn by a horse.
KNOWIN'	Small amount; 'Just a wee knowin'.'
LARN	Teach, educate. 'We'll larn you a lesson.'

LARRY	Large delivery vehicle
LEATHER	Ladder. 'The window cleaner was left hangin' on the winda when his leather fell on him.'
LOCK	Quantity, amount.
LUCK	Look, behold.
MORR	Female parent.
MUTTON DUMMIES	Plimsolls, rubber shoes.
MARE	Bathroom or bedroom mirror.
MARLEY	Marble.
NEB	Nose.
NI	Now, this instant: 'We're ready ni.'
NOAN	Not any.
NORN	Northern.
NYRPS	Sources of annoyance. 'She gave me the nyrps.'
ORR	Other.
OUL	Not young but can also be used to mean aged, useful. 'I bought myself a bit of an oul coat.'
OXTERCOG	Assist, give physical help. 'We had to oxtercog him across the road.'
PARRITCH	Porridge.
PAHLE	Make progress with difficulty, limp. 'He's an oul pahle.'
PARLETIC	Stocious, intoxicated. (see rightly)
PAN LUCKIN'	Prodigiously fond of a fry.
PECHLIN'	walking
PENTH	Pennyworth.
PHUT	Three of them are in a yard.
QUENCH	Extinguish, put out
QUEUY	Affectionate term for person called Hugh.
RAR	Prefer.
RARE	Bring up, raise, educate.
RENCH	Rinse: 'I'm away to rench the dishes.'
RIGHTLY	See Parletic Also implies prospering: 'He's doin' rightly now'
ROSINER	Alcoholic drink.
SACK	Unwell
SAFT	Not hard, mild; 'It's a saft mornin' '
SCALDED	Bothered, badly burned, harassed, vexed: 'My heart's scalded.'
SCRAPINS	What has been left over, thin 'She's away to scrapins.'

SEEINAWA	C and A store in Belfast.
SEX	Hour before seven in Ballymena.
SHEUGH	Ditch
SKIFF	Slight shower of rain.
SKITE	Dart, move swiftly.
SPITTIN'	Starting to rain.
STOUR	Dust, commotion.
STOVIN'	See parletic.
PUKE	Stuck up, to be sick.
QUARE	Memorable, unusual.
TENT	Small amount: 'Could you lend me a wee tent of milk?'
THISSUS	Asks the question 'Can this be my stop?' or 'Is this where I get off?'
THRAPPLE	Throat.
THROW OFF	To be sick. Elsewhere in the British Isles people throw up.
THRAN	Awkward, clumsy, difficult, unco-operative.
THUNDERGUB	Loud voiced person.
TIG	Touch. 'We were playing tig.'
TRINKET	Gutter.
WEE	With, in the company of. 'Who was that I saw you wee?'
WHERRYEFIR	Enquiry, asks where the person addressed is going
WHEEZLE	Goes with being chesty, bronchial. 'He's very wheezley.'
WHINGIN'	Crying, show irritability: 'That child's always whingin'.'
YOUSENS	You, yourselves: 'Tell yousens oursens is ready.'